THE KANALY
CONCEPT

THE KANALY CONCEPT

Keys to Understanding, Accumulating, Preserving and
Enjoying Your Money

E. Deane Kanaly

Kendall/Hunt
Publishing Company
Dubuque, Iowa

Copyright © 1986 by E. Deane Kanaly

Library of Congress Catalog Card Number: 85–81751

ISBN 0–8403–3820–1

Printed in the United States of America

B   403820   01

CONTENTS

FOREWORD

As a business and finance writer I have interviewed and written about dozens of *so-called* financial planners. So-called? Many insurance agents, stock and bond brokers, oil and gas operators and others *call* themselves financial planners. It's a bad joke in my opinion. They hide the fact that they are really salespeople. There's nothing new about this trend. Years ago life insurance agents found that when they stopped putting words like Agent or Salesman on their calling cards and added *Counsellor,* they were able to get into more homes and offices where they could close more sales. I'm not sure about the ethics involved in these situations. I believe in truth-in-labels and doing business under the right name.

Unfortunately today's general public has been led to believe there's one kind of financial planner. Most are unaware there's no state or federal licensing of planners—no impartial, qualified accreditation agency—so anyone and everyone can call themselves one. Just about any and every salesperson does! There are a few so-called "professional" designations relating to financial planning. However, I am not impressed with initials used after an individual's name—in the area of financial planning. Granted, some individuals with designations are well qualified, honest and competent planners. But the sad truth is just about anyone can receive the right to use the initials. To prove the point I sent a check to a so-called "financial planning institute" and within a week

I received a fancy certificate evidencing my membership. No questions asked. I could have been a convict serving time for embezzlement, and the financial planning institute would not have known and obviously not even cared. The main issue at the institution was probably "Will this guy's check clear?"

Deane Kanaly is a member of the elite class of what I call bona fide financial counsellors. These are *true* professionals offering no product for sale and no service other than counsel and advice. Deane, by the way, wears no initials after his name. Certainly his education, background and years of experience qualify him for membership in any honest professional society dedicated to financial planning. Some day there may actually be such a professional society. In the meantime, Deane is not trying to fool anyone or impress others by claiming to be a certified member of some organization of questionable integrity.

Clients of the Kanaly Trust Company are given quality advice following hours of consultation and review. The Company doesn't use formulas, but rather it treats each client as an individual. If insurance, stocks or other investments are recommended, the client acquires these through agents of the client's choosing. If a will or trust is recommended, the client selects the attorney or advisor to consult. This way the client knows he is getting sound, professional advice—not a sales pitch.

Deane is especially well qualified for the work he does. His background in banking, trusts and investments prepared him for the services he provides hundreds of individual and corporate clients. This book is a reflection of the man and his knowledge. He speaks clearly and directly.

The Kanaly Trust Company is more than just a state-chartered, financially secure corporation. It is a family business involving Deane, Mrs. Kanaly and their three sons. But it's no mom-and-pop outfit. Kanaly Trust employs several dozen professionals and staff people. They manage more than $250,000,000.

Over the years many clients and friends of the Kanalys have encouraged Deane to gather together his thoughts, ideas and theories and put them into book form. Following a public speech or seminar many attendees flock to the podium asking Deane to recommend books or other sources where they can learn more about the subjects Deane speaks on. So, this book is a compendium of years of experience and a lifetime of work. Reading it is like interviewing with Deane. He shares his thoughts, opinions and ideas just as if he were visiting in your office or living room. He would not expect you to agree with everything he says or believes. He wants you to *think* about those things. After careful study, reflection and research he wants you to reach your own conclusions. Sometimes, I suspect, he throws in a statement or comment designed to cause question or discussion. From time to time he'll give the interviewer or reader a *shock treatment;* he's jolting the other party into thinking about the point made. Deane has told me more than one time, "When I get people to *think* about wealth, money, the family, their futures, the next generations and how it all relates to aspects of living, then I feel I have provided a worthwhile service." Like Aristotle and Plato of centuries past Deane Kanaly asks that you think and act on these important matters. "How do you know that you know?" asks wise men. *Let's reason together* is the plea of thinkers.

Deane Kanaly would like to see millions of Americans intelligently consider the subjects of wealth, money, inheritances, lifestyles, charitable giving and dozens of other subjects detailed between the covers of this book. He wants to open new avenues of thought and create arenas for intelligent discussion—especially within the family unit. He's truly a financial counsellor's counsellor. He's honestly concerned about those millions of Americans who will inherit billions of dollars. He's not so interested that they will use those fortunes to buy this or that product but that the money be used wisely to enhance the lifestyles, pleasures and levels of satisfaction of present and future generations.

Largent Parks, Jr.
Dallas, Texas

Chapter One

THE PAST IS (PROBABLY) NOT PROLOGUE

—Apologies to William Shakespeare

I begin with a premise: The economic history of the United States during the past fifty years, and especially during the years since World War II, is *not* a valid guide for what is likely to occur in the future. At best, the past half-century will be of limited usefulness so far as personal financial planning is concerned.

Why?

Because I believe we are presently in a period of economic transition, marked by dramatic and frequently rapid changes. Furthermore, many of these changes are deeply rooted in our society; they are social and political alterations as well as economic, and, in effect, these drastic shifts are remaking America.

It is useful to examine some of these more important changes for several reasons. First, many of the ideas presented subsequently in this book are based on the assumption of these changes being real and meaningful. Second, looking at these changes and developments as they are occurring can give us valuable insight into what our futures will be like.

For convenience and as a way of getting a handle on what has happened and what is occurring, I propose to group these change elements into two categories: Economic Development and Social Trends. However, this rather artificial division should not mask the fact that these trends are all interrelated.

As we look at them we will find ourselves criss-crossing back and forth from time to time.

You may ask why not a grouping for *political* changes? The answer is that in our modern society political changes are almost always a reflection of the social and/or economic changes preceding them. The society or the economy undergoes some form of fundamental change or trauma, and in time—usually a very short time—the political processes catch up with the effects of the change or trauma. For example, it is likely we would not have a Social Security system had the nation not experienced a deep and protracted economic depression during the 1930's.

ECONOMIC DEVELOPMENTS

The shift from an industrial society to a services/information society. Of the many changes taking place in the United States during the last fifty years none is more far reaching in its impact and implication than our changing economy. We are moving rapidly and rather painfully from an industrial society, i.e., a society in which most of us *made* things, to a post-industrial one in which most of us will provide services or we will generate and distribute information.

In his provocative and perceptive book, *Megatrends**, author John Naisbett identifies some ten major shifts (or Megatrends, as he calls them) and says, "None is more subtle, yet more explosive, than the shift from an industrial to an information society." The shift from industrial to service is his first Megatrend.

Despite the great amount of publicity and attention which the post-industrial society has received from academics and government over the past few years, the idea is not entirely a new one. The megatrend shift emerged in the mid-1950's–1956, to be precise. That was a banner year for American industry. Automobile sales were setting records, and most of the indices of our industrial might were at or near their all-time highs. It was in 1956 that the number of white-collar workers first exceeded their blue-collar counterparts. Naisbett again: "Outwardly, the United States appeared to be a thriving industrial economy, yet a little noticed symbolic milestone heralded the end of an era: in 1956, for the first time in American history, white-collar workers in technical, managerial and clerical positions outnumbered blue-collar workers. Industrial America was giving way to a new society, where, for the first time in history, most of us worked with information rather than in industry."

---

*John Naisbett, *Megatrends, Ten New Directions Transforming Our Lives,* Warner Books, New York, 1982.

PRIOR PREDICTIONS PROVING PROLOGUES
ARE NOT PERFECT OR PREFERABLE FOR PLANNING

Adolph Hitler predicted his Third Reich would rule the world for a thousand years. Instead he spent ten years making a mess of Europe only to find the world wasn't ready for him. While Hitler was shouting about the next ten centuries, the Titanic was christened as the world's first unsinkable ship. The launching of the ill-fated Titanic occurred about the same time Henry M. Warner of Warner Bros. Pictures' fame in California was making a convincing argument against making movies with sound. "Who the hell wants to hear actors talk?" he asked.

Going back one hundred years, Lord Kelvin of the prestigious London think tank—The Royal Society—declared, without a degree of hesitation of course, that "Heavier than air flying machines are utterly impossible." And that was that so far as Lord Kelvin and the Royal Society were concerned. A few years later, in 1899 to be exact, Charles H. Duell was quoted as saying: "Everything that can be invented has been invented." It took a lot of nerve for Duell to make such a bold prediction since, at that point in history, he was Director of the U.S. Patent Office.

And then there was the Nobel Prize winner, Robert Millikan, who said in 1923, "There's no likelihood man can ever tap the power of the atom." They didn't take back the Nobel Prize, but he never won awards for accurate forecasting. Grover Cleveland may not go down in history as the greatest president or predictor of all times, but a lot of women remember it was Cleveland who said, "Sensible and responsible women do not want to vote." And last, but certainly not least, the sports fans of the world will remember Tris Speaker's words of wisdom at the time Babe Ruth changed jobs. The year was 1921: "Ruth made a big mistake when he gave up pitching." All these erroneous statements serve to prove one can't predict the future based on current and past events.

The 1956 shift has been accelerating during the past 30-plus years, creating an ever-widening gap between white-collars and blue-collars.

The post-industrial society was given another shove forward in 1957, one year later. This megatrend was much more widely noticed. The Soviet Union launched Sputnik. That event not only galvanized what has become known as the Space Race between the United States and the U.S.S.R., but it also led during the ensuing 25 years to satellite communications and to what Naisbett and Daniel Bell at Harvard call the "globalization of the information revolution."

A distinction is in order here. Naisbett's post-industrial society is primarily an information-oriented one, i.e., one in which most people will generate and distribute information as their principal economic activity. But information alone, in my view, is not solely what the post-industrial society

3

will be about. The provision of *services* will be at least as important. While I agree that information is crucial, I feel obliged to point out that information is always produced about *something,* and those somethings are likely to be economic activities, including the production of a multitude of services ranging from banking to fast foods and from inventory control to airline ticketing.

In addition, I believe that the United States for a variety of important economic and non-economic reasons will not be phasing-out of the production of steel, automobiles, machine tools, farm implements and machinery, and petrochemicals. In short, the economic shift to information and services, while it may be fundamental, will certainly not be absolute or total. It is important to keep this in mind so that the shift to the post-industrial society can be kept in proper perspective.

A common problem with the present-day financial reasoning of many Americans is what I call the fallacy of straight-line thinking. We see it often in the world of finance, especially among less sophisticated investors. Consider these two examples of ill-conceived straight-line "logic" and the unpleasant results.

First, consider *inflationary* straight-line mentality. As we look back we plainly see that during the 1970's our economy experienced substantial rates of annual inflation. It was the norm for workers to receive annual salary increases of 10% to 20% based on *increases in the cost of living*—another term for inflation. When applying straight-line thinking to inflation and using the past as a guide for the future, persons caught up in the straight-line way of reasoning *assume* future cost-of-living increases will climb at the same rate as in the past. They draw a straight line from a point in the past to a point representing the present. Next, the line is extended or continued in a straight line to some future point. "Wow!" exclaims today's straight-liner, "I'll be earning $500,000 a year by the time I reach retirement!" Don't believe it.

Another clear example of straight-line reasoning is found in the matter of residential real estate values. During the 1970's home values escalated— right along with inflation, cost-of-living and incomes. I am afraid some straight-line thinkers are buying real estate today with the expectation that the rates of increase will continue for the next twenty years at the same pace they have in the recent past. These people are envisioning million-dollar properties where the true price today may be closer to $100,000. How much will today's $100,000 home bring in five or ten years? Will residential real estate prices continue to escalate at the same rate as in the past five to ten years? Who knows? Probably not.

The fallacy of straight-line thinking is becoming clear to many of today's workers and investors. In some industries, such as airlines, salaries are actually decreasing. Labor contracts are being negotiated *downward* instead of upward as was the case for so many years. In some parts of the United States residential real estate prices are softening. Some homes that easily attracted $150,000 offers in recent times are today going begging at $125,000 or less.

4

The price of gold is one more clear example of potentially disastrous results from erroneous straight-line thinking. During the past few years the price of gold escalated from $100 an ounce to $250, then $500 and even $800. Many investors, mostly amateurs, bought gold with the idea that the price would move on to $1,000 and then to $2,000. Instead, the straight line peaked and gold prices fell almost as rapidly as they had increased, until finding a bottom at the $300 range. Ask any 1970's gold bug about straight-line thinking.

I shall always remember the client with more than $18 million tied up in a single issue of stock. His well-meaning accountants and others reminded him that the stock had, for the prior years, enjoyed an annual rate of growth of 20% to 30%. "At that rate, your portfolio will double every few years," his accountants reassured him. The stock was going for $78. At the same time his financial counsellor recommended the portfolio be diversified. However, this advice landed on the deaf ears of a dedicated straight-line thinker. Less than a year later the man considered himself lucky because he was able to get out of the stock as the price was sliding through the $30 range!! He was $10 million poorer and had come to regard himself as an *ex*-straight-line-thinking investor.

Caution: Don't inadvertently fall into the traps surrounding the "logic" of straight-line thinking. It's been the undoing of many a stockmarket player, commodity trader, real estate investor and careless financial planner.

As we continue thinking in terms of Naisbett's Megatrends let's keep in mind the important distinctions between an industrial economy and a services/information-oriented economy and the *strategic materials* required. Whereas the critical inputs for an industrial economy are primarily capital and labor, those for a services/information society are *knowledge* and labor. In modern high-tech industries, access is provided primarily by know-how and brain power. If those two ingredients, plus a market or need are present, experience suggests that the capital will be made available.

What does the shift to a post-industrial society mean then in terms of individual economic activity and, ultimately, to personal financial planning?

Because of easier access and lower capital requirements we would expect to see a new generation of entrepreneurs emerge, and that is precisely what is taking place. In 1950 we were creating less than 100,000 new businesses a year; today, despite the most protracted recession since World War II, we are creating more than 600,000 annually. That represents *real* growth, even when we recognize that our present economy is many times larger than it was 34 years ago.

The services/information economy with the new entrepreneuralism implies widespread decentralization, and it is no coincidence that this is also a Naisbett Megatrend, the fifth of his ten, to be exact.

I believe we will witness several other marked economic changes, one of which will be slower economic growth. While the growth will be at a slower rate, it will be of a higher quality than we have known in the past. It will be based to a large extent on savings rather than consumption, on living more within our means and on making products which are better and designed to last longer. The current emphasis on quality control and after-sale service in the U.S. automobile industry is no passing fancy; it will be here just as long as European and Japanese competition is present. Meaning it is here to stay. To be sure, this is a trend to be encouraged, but the transition will not be painless. It has enormous implications for personal financial planning.

Feeding this slower economic growth will be smaller economic subsidies from the Federal government, although total governmental economic aid may be expected to increase as governmental services move from Washington to the state capitals.

I suspect we will also see a continued wringing-out of inflation from our economy as economic growth slows. Economic growth will have to be real, i.e., financial expansion will have to come from increased production of information, goods and services rather than from the notorious bandit known as inflation. This fact of economic life has enormous implications for your economic planning and future well being.

And we are going to bear witness to a phenomenon which has no precedent in the past fifty years, or throughout history for that matter: During the remainder of this century we are going to witness millions of people inheriting billions of dollars. These dollars will come from at least three sources: (1) benefits provided by employers, the government or the people themselves; (2) inflation in real estate values resulting in larger estates passing to next generations; and (3) the sale of thousands of successful individual businesses. The availability of these dollars—again—will have an enormous impact on our personal financial lives. Indeed, when millions inherit billions there will be considerable effect upon our economy, government programs, employment, consumption and investment.

Finally, and perhaps most important, we will witness a shift to greater self-reliance in personal and economic matters than we've seen in the recent past. But more about that later. For now, let's continue examining some of these economic developments in greater detail.

Slower economic growth. This phenomenon is already underway and is coupled with the decline in inflation. I will leave it to learned economists to determine precisely what rate or rates of growth are required to sustain our living standards and political stability, but it is safe to say we will not enjoy economic growth rates as high as those we've had during the four decades since World War II. Occasionally we fail to accurately judge the rate of economic growth we are presently in or the rate of the recent past.

Many years ago a former employer of mine underwrote a detailed study which subsequently proved to be a real eye-opener for me. The study covered the 30-year period from 1923 to 1953. It addressed the question of whether an executive would have been better off financially to have owned rather than rented his home. As you can imagine, back in the late 1950's when the study

6

was made, it would have been a natural assumption to *know* the correct answer. With residential real estate values strong at the time and renting one's home considered a rather unpopular choice, I along with many fellow employees were more than mildly surprised when we learned the outcome of the study. That's correct. The study proved beyond a shadow of a doubt that a executive would have been dollars ahead had he opted to *rent* instead of own his home during the 30 years covered by the study! However, had any of us made a financial decision in the late 1950's based on this study and elected to rent instead of own a home for the next 30 years, we would have made a colossal monetary blunder. That past is *not* prologue, and this isolated case serves to prove the point.

One can point to an entire spectrum of reasons which add up to lower growth rates, most of which are familiar. The following are some of the more important reasons:

1. The worldwide rise in oil prices has transferred an almost incalculable amount of our national wealth to other countries, especially to those in the Middle East. And while oil prices appear to have stabilized, at least as this is written, the fact is that in early 1985 oil was still priced somewhere between seven and eight times its pre-1973 levels. Net result: the enormous amounts of capital that would have otherwise been available to fuel U.S. economic growth are now building power plants in Venezuela, apartment houses in Iran and airports in Saudi Arabia.

2. Foreign competition in virtually all our basic industries has been stepped up dramatically during the past ten years, and there is no sign that it will let up. We are already seeing a shrinkage of some of our basic industries, steel being the most notable example, and this trend will continue. Maybe you have not given much thought as to why we are no longer Number One in steel. Consider the following as an illustration of one of many reasons:

I don't know if you are old enough to remember the year 1945. That was a time for great celebration in the United States. World War II ended. The Allies had defeated the Axis. We had devastated Germany and Japan and forced these aggressors into unconditional surrender. But, what obviously never occurred to anyone at that time was that in defeating Germany and Japan, we had laid the groundwork for the ultimate handicap of our domestic steel industries. You see, at the end of the great war, Japan and Germany had no choice but to totally rebuild their factories. While new steel plants were going up in Japan and Germany, here in the United States we happily continued to operate our 1920-vintage plants. It never seemed to occur to anyone that these U.S. plants were outdated and rapidly becoming even more obsolete thanks to the dramatic post-war technological revolution under way.

The United States won the war, but in so doing, lost—at least for the foreseeable future—the international steel battle. Germany's and Japan's post-war industrial complexes are now so superior we find the U.S. at a serious disadvantage in the competitive worldwide markets as well as right here at home. It's more economical for American corporations to import steel, and other products, than to buy from our own stateside plants!

We now see a similar situation at the U.S. household level. The typical American accentuates the expedient and the immediate, while carelessly over-looking the long-term impact of his or her action, or lack of action. As in the case of our national steel industry, today's household fails to understand the critical importance of handling accumulated capital. In many cases these in-dividuals are completely overlooking the purposes for which capital was ac-cumulated in the first place. During the boom years following World War II the American industry enjoyed years of apparent prosperity while failing to plan ahead. Today the typical American is saving for the future (witness the billions of dollars flowing annually into IRA's, for example) but the question remains: Does the saver know how to protect and preserve the capital being saved? Does he or she know how to make the capital as productive as possible? Let's hope the typical American doesn't inadvertently fall into the same traps and make the same basic errors as U.S. industry did. Let's hope the individual investor will prove to be superior in his capital understanding and a better fiscal planner than our nation's industrial leadership has been.

3. Our savings rate is deemed to be among the lowest of the world's indus-trialized nations. In contrast, the savings rate hovers at about 15% in West Germany and 25% in Japan. We simply have not formed capital at a rate sufficiently high enough to sustain our historical growth rates.
4. Productivity gains will be more difficult to achieve as the U.S. economy shifts from an industrial base to a more service/information-oriented one. Productivity improvements have depended on large capital increases and infusion of new capital. Capital-caused productivity will be more difficult to achieve in service/information industries and more expensive.

Note also that three of these developments are not short-term or tem-porary in character. High energy costs, foreign competition and slower pro-ductivity gains are likely to be with us a long, long time.

Smaller relative economic expenditure at the Federal government level. It is very difficult to make predictions in this area because of conflicting trends within the Federal government itself. On one hand, we have the let's-get-the-government-out-of-our-lives movement set in motion by the Reagan admin-istration. This effort gained considerable momentum during his first term and, in my view, reflects a deeply-held belief on the part of many Americans that Washington—in the name of civil rights, economic justice, or whatever one chooses to call it—has simply intruded itself too far into our personal lives.

8

On the other hand, we have the enormous budget commitments to entitlement programs and national defense. Large budgets equate to correspondingly high deficits. Public opinion indicates an increased awareness of the hazards of bigger budgets and deficits. Budgets and deficits show signs of steadily increasing, not decreasing as the Reagan administration promised. So, we are dealing with the *net* effect of the Federal government's enormous and ever-growing economic demand. How long and how large is unpredictable.

It may be more useful, therefore, to address Washington's economic demand in those areas closely related to personal financial well being, such as the so-called entitlement programs, Social Security and the host of income-redistribution programs which Washington currently administers. I believe many of these programs will be reduced or eliminated or transferred to state government, and the Federal government's economic demand *relative to the Gross National Product* will shrink.

What these developments will lead to, in my judgment, is a new set of government tax and investment policies designed to encourage savings and discourage excessive debt. For example, we are likely to see the tax deductibility of loan interest reduced or eliminated, including that for certain types of mortgage interest.

We have already witnessed the beginning of the shift of certain welfare, income-supplement and food distribution and health programs to the states; the shift is likely to continue because—again—it reflects many people's conviction that they need to get the Feds out of their lives.

I call this emerging set of governmental policies and practices the New Federalism and see it resting firmly on three basic concepts:

1. That the private sector, including individuals, will have to assume a larger proportionate share of economic and social services, including jobs, life and health insurance, income and retirement benefits.
2. That economic and tax policies that encourage saving and discourage excessive consumption and debt will be put into place; and
3. That state and local governments will have to assume a larger share of the economic burden of social, income and welfare programs.

This isn't to say, of course, that the Federal government will abandon entirely its commitments to economic and social welfare. Far from it. I do argue, however, that those commitments will gradually shift to the private sector and state and local governments. Thus, the Fed's *share* will diminish.

No discussion of the "New Federalism" would be complete without a few words concerning our tottering Social Security system. Here I choose to focus on the individual and tell the reader exactly what I advise my clients.

Regardless of the much-publicized actions taken to "save" Social Security, the system remains in precarious financial condition for three fundamental reasons—one economic, one social, and the third political.

9

First, the system is paying out more dollars than it takes in. Clearly that cannot continue indefinitely.

Second, the ratio of the number of people being carried by Social Security is rising relative to the number of people doing the carrying, i.e., those who are paying for it. In 1936 when the system was established there were 75 workers paying into Social Security for each person receiving benefits from it. Today there are only two workers to support each person receiving benefits.

Third—and this is the threshold consideration in my view—the political process simply will not deal responsibly with the issue of accruals needed to maintain Social Security's financial health. Put another way, Congress will refuse to raise the FICA tax to the levels required. Doing so would be predictably a very unpopular political move. At best look for Congress to, at least in part, fund Social Security from general revenues.

It is important to remember what Social Security is and what it is not. Unfortunately, too many of us have been brainwashed into thinking of Social Security as a guaranteed retirement *insurance* plan. In no sense of the word should we ever think of Social Security as insurance or as being guaranteed. There's no policy; there's no contractual agreement, and the plan is not based on sound actuarial principles (three important ingredients of any insurance scheme). Social Security fails to even come close to my dictionary's definition of a guarantee. Congress passed the Social Security Act fifty years ago, and just about every Congress since has tampered with the law in some fashion or another. It is important to recognize that the next Congress *could* toss the whole thing out the window. Of course, I am not predicting the demise of Social Security, and so long as we send politicians instead of statesmen to Washington, you can bet your bottom dollar Congress will continue to view Social Security as a tool for guaranteed re-election. No one denies that Social Security is bankrupt or that the plan is getting financially worse by the year. In spite of recent large increases in Social Security taxes, the fund continues to go deeper and deeper into red ink.

It is becoming more and more obvious that too many so-called intelligent Americans are building plans for retirement on a Social Security base. I say this because less than 30% of American taxpayers who are eligible for an Individual Retirement Account (IRA) have taken advantage of this tax-advantaged law designed to enable the individual to establish his or her own retirement plan. Seventy percent of the population is ignoring or overlooking the advantages of IRA's. Obviously a large portion of these people are thinking Social Security is going to be around and will play a substantial role in their retirement incomes. Of course, some of the 70% may simply not be thinking at all.

At the risk of sounding like a proponent for additional Big Brother-type legislation—that is, favoring laws *making* us do for ourselves those things that we know we should do voluntarily—maybe there should be laws obligating us to provide for our retirements. We have become accustomed to state laws requiring us to own personal liability insurance or demonstrate financial responsibility in order to operate a motor vehicle on the public streets and highways. Such laws, of course, are designed to protect third parties from loss resulting from our carelessness. If all citizens were required to show personal, individual responsibility for their own futures, it seems just as reasonable as being obligated to look out for the welfare of others! Why aren't more Americans concerned about their financial futures? Are they counting on Uncle Sam to take care of them? Has the welfare-state mentality become so entrenched in our modern society that we have lost our individual concern for our own welfare?

The lesson for all Americans is clear: Social Security is something we all need to be concerned about, but for heaven's sake let's not count on it to provide a significant portion of our retirement income. My best guess is that the money will not be there, at least not in the amounts to which retirees will believe they are entitled when the time comes to collect.

Diminished inflation rates. I believe inflation rates will come down over the long term as more people perceive that we cannot look to inflation to produce economic growth. If the Federal government's economic demand relative to GNP shrinks, as I believe it will, inflationary pressures should be significantly eased.

Furthermore, if people begin to perceive that future dollars are not likely to be materially cheaper than present ones, they will be less encouraged to borrow now and pay later. Savings will increase, capital will be generated, investment will accelerate and real economic growth will be the net result.

Millions of people will inherit billions of dollars. This is a scenario which will be played out during the next several decades. It is a revolutionary socioeconomic phenomenon never before witnessed. Its implications are neither well recognized nor easily understood. These billions of dollars will come from several sources: the home, businesses, insurance, personal, company and government benefit programs.

Dual career families will proliferate. The phenomena of two careers in one family will have a growing impact on investment, consumption and basic political and economic thinking. If you think about the combination of the dual income, together with inheritance on one or both sides of the marriage, you can understand how this is bound to change people's attitude and motivation towards money and the things money buys as well as savings patterns.

No one has a very good "handle" on exactly how many dollars will be involved. It can be said with certainty that the number will be astronomical, and as these dollars find their way into the mainstream of the economy they will have an enormous impact not only on our personal lives but will greatly affect our social outlook as well.

Which brings me to the second category we must consider—Social Trends. If we are to gain any insight into the kind of America and world for which we have to make our plans and in which we will live out our financial futures, we must recognize and understand the role played by Social Trends.

SOCIAL TRENDS

The striving for personal identity. In my opinion the most important and pervasive social factor affecting our American society today is the individual's struggle to establish and maintain personal identity. We live in a world increasingly characterized by a mechanical, computer-generated, mass-market approach to everything from the womb to the tomb.

The signs are everywhere around us—from the printed T-shirts to "designer" clothing ironically bearing someone else's initial or name to customized automobiles and uniquely-designed homes. All these symbols cry out, "Look! I'm Me! I'm Somebody!" I will leave it to the sociologists to make detailed value judgments about these trends. My guess is that on balance it is a healthy and restorative one in that it restates and reminds us of a precept on which this country was founded, indeed a basic trend common to Western civilized thought: the individual *is* unique and counts for something, perhaps everything.

To be sure, some of the more obvious manifestations of this drive for indentity are frequently vulgar or, at best, just plain silly. It has helped make egalitarianism a form of secular religion. I must admit that in a milieu where one man's opinion, *per se,* is as good as another's, regardless of the subject under discussion, individualism is not always conducive to elevating the quality of life.

Yet, there is an undercurrent of something else here, something which reenforces the individual's striving for identity. This "something" might be described as a growing recognition of—or commitment to—"quality" as being a necessary part of our lives.

The retreat from "More-ism." I call this trend the retreat from "More-ism," by which I mean that more and more of us are recognizing and making the distinctions between personal economic growth in a purely quantitative sense and personal progress in a qualitative one. The 25 to 35 year olds getting married and forming households today are less likely than their parents were to measure their success and personal fulfillment solely in terms of the growth in their income and assets. This younger generation is not indifferent to quantitative growth, but their approach, it seems to me, is more balanced and optimistic. Their childhood and formative years were more secure, at least materially, than were those of their parents. The senior generation's childhoods were indelibly and understandibly marked by the Great Depression of the 1930's. Rightly or wrongly, our new adults take material growth almost as a given and tend to focus more on the quality of their lives.

Not so incidentally, the depression-shaped generation is maturing and dying off and is being replaced by generations that on the whole have a more optimistic, individual-oriented outlook. I believe this to be the case despite the fact that newer generations have lived in a world threatened by nuclear war and other assorted modern-day potential disasters.

The 100-year lifespan. Some of you may raise your eyebrows but I am convinced we are approaching the 100-year lifespan for many Americans. It is not here yet, but it would be well to think in terms of a century-long life and plan for it.

What is it likely to mean: For starters . . .

- Forget retirement. Anyone who lives for nearly 10 decades in reasonably good health will have more than one career. Probably several. Besides, it will be necessary from an overall economic and social perspective to lengthen the span of our working and producing years. Otherwise, we will have a lopsided society in which young and middle-aged people will be working in greater measure to support an ever-increasing population of senior—indeed, very senior—citizens!
- You will most likely have more than one marriage. Your spouse will likely die before you or perhaps you will find the notion of remaining with one mate for more than three-quarters of a century intolerable! That isn't too startling an idea when you consider that today more than one of every two marriages ends in divorce. The average marriage today lasts less than 20 years.
- Society will be stretched from its current three-generation span to four generations. The so-called "generation gap" will be even wider than in the past unless we can develop better ways to communicate between the generations. Such improved communication will not be merely a social or familial nicety. It will be a necessity if younger generations are to get more knowledge and wealth out of what the earlier generations worked so long and hard to accumulate.

Despite all these impending changes, some elements of our social lives will remain constant. The human condition will always be characterized by certain basic emotional needs, of which I count three.

There will always be **hope for gain.** It is, of course, more prominent among young people who are just beginning their working lives and starting their families. These young and hope-filled people will stress the quality of their lives more than did their predecessors. However, they will—indeed, will *have* to—pay attention to the growth of their incomes and assets as underpinnings for the quality they seek to attain for their lives.

Then there is the **fear of loss** that begins to appear in the individual once he has accumulated assets. The natural reaction is to begin taking steps to protect what has become our property. This emotion grows stronger as the nest egg grows. Most are not paranoid about protecting and preserving property, but it is normal to be concerned about keeping it. It's natural to believe that someday we will need it.

Finally, there is the **need for love, affection and respect** common to everyone. To be sure, these include both recognition and reward for our achievements. But this human need is also the "bottom line" to what life, work and struggle are all about. Without love, affection and respect life is rather empty and without meaning.

The task facing all of us is to find the way to measure and monitor our economic progress and balance this progress against future needs and desires. Then we lessen the fears, frustrations and insecurities that plague every one of us at one time or another. Fortunately, we now have the tools at the family and household level to accomplish this task.

IMPORTANT. Since new tax laws, regulations, and judgements occur daily, please refer to the tax bracket estimates and procedures as a working basis but not exact. Had I waited to verify all tax illustrations for current rulings this book could never have been written. No action should be taken without first consulting your tax advisor.

The remaining chapters are devoted to identifying and learning ways to use these tools and how to put them to work in building a lifestyle that makes you and your family happy while providing a peace-of-mind environment.

In short, the goal is to make you feel good about yourself. Forget the past. Now is the time to discuss your Personal Financial Life Cycle and to learn how to integrate it into your future.

Chapter Two

THE PERSONAL FINANCIAL LIFE CYCLE

Through my experiences while working with thousands of people of all ages, various income strata and at differing levels of assets accumulation, a personal financial life cycle became apparent. This financial life cycle is best illustrated as an hourglass (Chart 2.1).

Our education, inheritance, talents, energy, background and experience comprise the basic elements with which we move through the cycle. These factors affect our ability to cope with our economic existence and to alter the ultimate outcome of our personal financial evolvement.

My experience indicates there is *not* a direct correlation between the degree of one's success and the amount of education, inheritance, talent or even experience. The one single ingredient that runs through and is a key part of the makeup of successful people I have known and worked with is the amount of energy they possess. Energy breeds enthusiasm just as enthusiasm begets energy. It's the old chicken-and-egg situation. One leads to the other, and together energy and enthusiasm form the basis through which people apply their educations, inheritances, talents and experiences in a successful formula for living. I'm not referring to just financial success but also to truly enjoyable living. Considering the varying degrees of concentration and densities in the sands of the hourglass, I visualize five basic financial periods in everyone's economic life: Formation, Orientation, Survival, Accumulation and Preservation.

Kanaly Trust Company

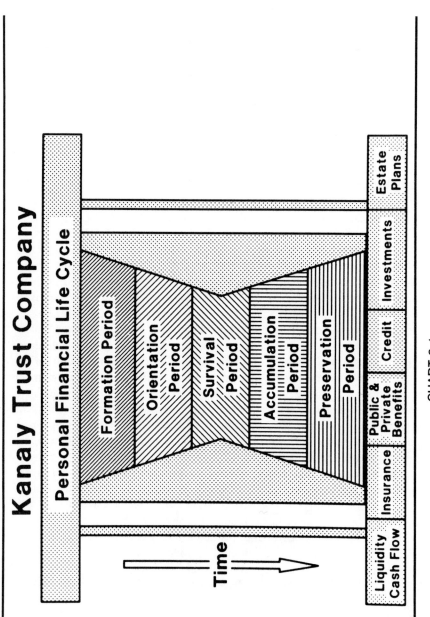

Personal Financial Life Cycle

Formation Period

Orientation Period

Survival Period

Accumulation Period

Preservation Period

Time

Liquidity Cash Flow | Insurance | Public & Private Benefits | Credit | Investments | Estate Plans

CHART 2.1

FORMATION

The first period is common to all of us. Formation is the time when we start accumulating our basic needs. It is the time in which we are completing our formal education, beginning our careers and becoming involved in marriage and child bearing. We begin to see the formation of the six elements of personal finance and the obvious need for developing good financial habits which, if implemented correctly, will prevail for a lifetime. Our liquidity and cash flow during this period are automatic in terms of their evolvement. We have very little liquidity. Our cash-flow planning is finite because we are literally determining how and when we shall pay the utility bills, department store bills and the rent—typically on the first or the fifteenth of the month. Our budgeting is as exact and accurate an element in our personal and financial life as it will ever be. Our insurance is probably adequate but minimal. The lowest cost term life insurance prevails in most situations. We are contributing to our public and private benefit plans simply because it is the law or because contributions are being made automatically by our employer. Much of the discretionary contributions to be made by the employee are overlooked or are a foregone conclusion at this period thanks to other cash requirements which seemingly have higher precedence. Our credit usage is mainly limited to consumer debt: paying off the wedding rings, paying for the birth of children, paying for furniture, household appliances and automobiles through an extensive use of consumer credit, also known as monthly payments. Investment debt during this period, generally speaking, is at a minimum. Investments are nominal—concentrated mainly in equity in a condominium or house and/or contributions to employer benefit plans. Our estate plans are very simple if, indeed, a plan of any sort exists. Very simple wills are the tone of estate planning during the formation period. This portion of the cycle is occasioned by a "must do" personal financial formula. We are, as a rule, doing what we must do to provide for basic human needs: food, housing, clothing and transportation.

ORIENTATION

From the formation period we move into a period of life in which we become oriented to better understanding our talents and recognizing our backgrounds relative to others. We start defining our objectives and goals a bit more clearly. This is when the children are between the pediatrician and the orthodontist, the lowest cost our offspring will ever be while they are members of our household. Our income has usually grown from what it was during the formation period, particularly in two-income-earning households.

Income tax begins to be a growing factor in the family's overall consideration during this period; taxes are higher and income is bracketing up substantially.

During the orientation period much of our liquidity and cash-flow commitments, as well as credit obligations, are made to differing types of investments. Tax shelters which are designed to reduce income taxation enter our economic scene. In my experience too little cognizance is given to the fact that the use of liquidity and the tying up of cash flow and credit during this period will often provide serious limitations in terms of what the individual or family *should* be doing, or *may* do, in the next period of their financial existence. During the latter part of this cycle we are seeing a great deal of career adjustment, i.e., people leaving one job for another simply because they have found themselves cash-flow poor and/or credit weary. They have little or no liquidity to sustain their expanding lifestyles and/or to service their debt commitments. Today we see up-front bonuses paid to lure an individual from one job to another. The bait is especially attractive when the recruited executive needs it to bail himself out of serious credit extension and/or crucial cash-flow impairments incurred by the excessive utilization of questionable tax shelters and other nonliquidable investments. When individuals get too much credit tied up in investments, such as limited partnerships or syndications, they are usually unable to wisely determine when to sell the investment. It doesn't seem to matter at that point whether it is a profitable investment or a loss situation. Without the ability to make a timely decision to liquidate a given investment they find themselves unable to meet ongoing cash-flow commitments. The liquidity having been used and credit extended, or even over-extended, they are unable to sustain other aspects of their financial life in a logical and adequate fashion, e.g., purchasing an additional home to satisfy a growing family's needs or to continue commitments to worthwhile employer benefit plans. Valuable social and economic investments are usually overlooked when the individual is unduly concerned and occupied by a liquidity crisis. Such pre-occupations are common in the orientation period.

SURVIVAL

The next position in the evolving personal financial life cycle is what I refer to as the survival period. This is a time in which the fulcrum often swings towards either a successful, ongoing financial future or a very seriously limited one. This is a period in which the *net* cash flow is at a minimum for most individual and family situations. It is when we are undertaking to educate our children, live in the biggest home possible, exercise stock options, contribute to employer benefit plans, and perhaps help elderly parents or other handicapped members of the family. When my family was in our survival period, my wife used to say, "We can do all the big things but we can't buy shoe laces." The cash flow or cash crunch seems more limited than even during the formation period, our initial financial phase. We have feelings of "not getting anywhere" and during the survival period we begin to wonder whether or not we're on the right track, at least from a financial point of view. Understanding and recognizing these obstacles afford us opportunities to be better prepared for them if and when they are encountered. Then we can more easily accommodate the various needs of education, home, corporate benefits, stock options, business formation and family. Otherwise, we may inadvertently experience a lifestyle reversal. Such an unfortunate event occurs in many families due to poor presurvival planning. It is during our survival phase that we begin to see the serious need for the wise use of investment credit and certainly the evolvement of sophisticated financial and estate planning. The object is to survive the survival period with our financial head on straight. It's easier said than done.

ACCUMULATION

We move into the accumulation period around the early 50's of our chronological age. The children are gone. The house is usually too big. Lifestyle is set. Our incomes remain constant—maybe even continue to increase—and we notice discretionary income beginning to appear along with the need to make determinations for the accumulations of sound and wise investments. Generally speaking, I have noticed this is the first period in which people really begin to accumulate and to make substantial discretionary investments. Some say this is when life begins. It's when most individuals become "retirement conscious." If, for the first three periods of the cycle they have *only* been able to accumulate an equity in their home, build a cash reserve, educate their children, help elderly parents and contribute to their employer and private benefit plans, most feel they have made *no* substantial financial gains. However, the fact is they have done well but may not realize how far they have progressed at this point. Achieving this should be highly satisfying.

During the accumulation period they will begin to experience a new form of income—discretionary income. The need to identify *discretionary* investments which will further secure their advancing years is the goal of the individual in the accumulation phase of the cycle. Some tell me the accumulation period is their happiest and most rewarding phase of the total financial cycle.

During the accumulation period we observe various interesting forms of behavior and conduct. For example, medical doctors will not, as a general rule, argue with the accepted concepts that our physical health and well-being is directly affected by our financial health. Of course, a case can easily be made for the reverse: Favorable financial status stimulates good physical and mental conditions. The well-balanced individual is one who develops and maintains a healthy body and an alert mind and one who operates on a sound financial foundation. He or she lives in a financially comfortable environment. This occurs when the healthy person feels good about what he has (income, assets, plans for the future) and is able to enjoy the material things in life without feelings of guilt or experiencing other discomforting emotions—either real or imagined.

How many times have you known of a person who suffered financial reverses only to shortly thereafter incur a disabling physical or mental impairment? If the truth were known, the financial failure and the physical and/or mental setbacks may have occured in tandem, with the financial portion of the equation becoming obvious before the physical. I recall an Oklahoma bank executive who suffered severe financial reverses early in 1983. He died of cancer in mid–1985. His doctor told me the autopsy revealed the death-dealing cancer probably had its origins early in the year 1983—the exact time the now-deceased man became aware of his deteriorating financial condition. In many cases these types of instances boil down to a chicken-and-egg equation. Some argue that the physical or mental illness *causes* financial reversals; others make a case for the opposite cause and effect. What is important, it seems to me, is my observation that when my clients maintain a sound financial plan and perspective along with a good physical or mental exercise regime, they seem to fare well in *all* aspects of their lives. I have witnessed cases where a person became unduly worried and concerned about a personal matter, usually related in one way or another to finance or money, and shortly thereafter began showing signs of physical or mental problems. In many of these instances, *apparent* financial reverses followed.

I'll leave it up to the professionals in medicine, including the psychiatrists, to demonstrate the cause and effect relationships between our mind, our body and our financial status. To me it's not as important to know which of the trio is more likely to trigger a breakdown in another—because as individuals these occurrences are not likely to follow patterns but rather to occur differently in individual cases. What's important is knowing and acting upon the fact that the mind, body and finances are intertwined. You'll likely become keenly aware of these mind-body-finance relations during the latter phases of the accumulation cycle. Knowing and understanding these relationships will enable you to perform at maximum levels in the final portion of the Financial Life Cycle—the preservation period.

PRESERVATION

The preservation period of our financial life cycle is when we begin to think in terms of protecting what we have accumulated and making our assets as productive as possible for the purposes for which we accumulated them. This is a period of beginning to arrange or even rearrange our investments from those types of assets that we use to accumulate property to those types of assets which are more desirable for protecting our property and producing alternative income. *Retirement income* is paramount in one's thinking and planning at this time. This is a period of decreasing use of borrowing for investment as well as the use of consumer credit. The preservation phase is a period of increasing interest in estate planning, a period of lessening needs in both liquidity and cash-flow requirements. More discernment is practical in the use of public and private benefit programs as well as cautious consideration of alternate forms of investments. In short—a time of caution.

HUMAN LIFE CYCLE/FINANCIAL LIFE CYCLE

Passive Income/Vocation Income

The entire personal financial life cycle, it seems, indicates that all of us should be, indeed *must be,* knowledgeable about our passive-income to vocation-income ratio. By that I mean income from investments such as rent, interest and dividends together with private pension plan payments, plus income later to be derived from IRA's and Keoghs as well as Social Security becomes a critical factor in the income stream. Obviously, as we pass through the financial life cycle the passive-income to vocation-income ratio should be increasing toward the passive side. Our vocation income eventually expires, as a rule, leaving only passive income for survival. Someday we will be unable or unwilling to work quite as hard to produce income for our needs in our lifestyle and for accumulation. Sooner or later everyone stops working and ceases producing income from labor!

Inheritance/Obligation

Is the individual or family facing potential inheritances from previous generations or facing potential financial obligations or both? This is a question requiring careful consideration in personal financial planning. If we have elderly parents or grandparents facing periods of dependency due to debilitating illnesses and/or extreme longevity of life when medical care costs usually become substantial and their resources are limited, then financial planning should be altered to accommodate this real or potential obligation in the family's financial picture. On the other hand, if inheritances are anticipated then the opposite ingredients are present allowing alternate financial plans for the family in this second posture. Both the amounts of financial responsibility as well as financial benefits through inheritance must be carefully estimated. This estimate must include the approximate time of receipt of the inheritance or distribution contemplated.

Hope for Gain / Fear of Loss

The first two phases, formation and orientation, as well as the early part of phase three, the survival period, are dominated by the human motivation of *hope for gain.* It is during these periods we are looking forward to "more"—more income and accumulation of more assets. In the latter part of the survival period through the accumulation and preservation periods, *fear of loss* begins to be an increasingly important motivational factor in our personal financial life cycle. Hope for gain remains an influential part of our motivation. We will probably continue to want more. However, we most certainly do not want to lose what we have accumulated, so at some point our basic motivation changes from hope for gain to fear of loss as we progress through the life cycle. Unfortunately, this metamorphosis can occasion a new series of insecure feelings. That is, if we are not extremely careful we can be so overly fearful of not having enough or losing what we have that we feel just as insecure and confused as we did in the earlier stages of our life cycle. This insecurity and confusion is exemplified in this sad but true story.

I shall never forget a remarkable situation which occurred many years ago. An elderly and childless widow who had no known relatives died. I was the trust officer of the organization which was executor of the woman's estate. I went to her apartment to inventory the furniture and personal belongings. What I found was an amazing record of austerity and frugality. Her husband, who'd passed away several years before, and the now-deceased wife, though worth three-quarters of a million dollars, had over the years hidden cash in clothing and bureau drawers. Money was stuffed in the sofa. Several thousand dollars cash was found in each of a dozen locations. The couple had never cashed traveler's checks left over from vacations taken many years ago. They owned thousands of dollars worth of Series E Bonds, all long past maturity. They had substantial amounts of money in checking accounts and low-interest savings accounts. They had all sorts of records dating back to the day of their marriage—many in crate boxes, along with three-by-five cards listing each check they had ever cashed and how it was spent. I found handwritten records of expenditures tallying to the total of each check listed on the small cards. I found the warranty on a sewing machine purchased from Sears & Roebuck before 1920. Their obvious insecurity and their quest to accumulate, along with their fear of owning a home were reflections of their obvious fears and concerns brought on by the 1930's depression. Those fears and ghosts of the past prevented them from enjoying a lifestyle commensurate with their accumulations and earnings.

The widow's lifestyle had deteriorated even further after her husband's death. Before his passing there was evidence of some travel and recreation. However it appeared she had hardly ventured out of her small apartment for years. Her estate eventually went to a foundation for the elderly and a children's hospital, in accordance with her last will and testament.

22

Their unreasonable fear of loss was clearly evident, and this unhealthy emotion dominated nearly all aspects of their lives. Their apartment was very modest. Their lifestyle was that of a low-income American couple struggling to survive on minimal resources.

The personal financial life cycle tracks our lifetime activities. In our youth we are full of dreams and anticipation, unaware of our own mortality and looking forward and in most instances, upward. We think about enhancing our income, improving our lifestyle, increasing our possessions. *Acquiring* dominates our thinking. As we mature physically as well as emotionally, we begin to reveal within our lifestyle choices in a clear definition of our physical and emotional needs. This is a time we often experience maximum stress in terms of responsibility in our vocations, in our family relations, in our community commitments. The survival period is more than just surviving financially; it's a period for surviving the tides of change in all phases of life. During the later portion of the survival period, the community begins to place more demands on the individual for financial aid and/or personal commitments for service. This is particularly true of an up-scale achiever. When we examine the survival period, we see our lives in a much broader context than simply financial. The same is true in the accumulation phase when the perceived guilt of our financial life becomes evident. Demands are competing with our desire to accumulate. These demands come from our church, our university, local health associations and charities. Everywhere we go and each way we turn it seems we feel we are not doing enough. We are made to feel guilty for our imagined neglect in terms of both time and money. *Guilt* becomes a major competitor for our innate desire to accumulate capital for our retirement years. We didn't have the opportunity in the prior period of survival because we had commitments to our family and to our career or profession. Now we have a new competitor for our desire to provide for ourselves and often the competition comes from the community at large.

As we progress through the early stages of the accumulation period and on to the beginning of the preservation period, our physical and emotional stamina suggest we can replace what we have should it become necessary to do so. We can replace our job; we can fail in a business and start another. We can move to another city to practice our profession or employment activities. But as we move toward the early phase of the preservation period and our physical and emotional activities begin to become more fixed and less flexible, we become concerned about our ability to replace lost income. Job and career changes become more feared than earlier. Apprehension sets in. The fear-of-loss syndrome becomes accentuated. The same is true of our spending habits. There may not be enough reserve for an advanced or prolonged life. Our own mortality becomes more evident. Mortality, that is, in the sense of death as well as our physical inability to "run as fast." To reproduce or replace what we have should we face substantial loss is next to impossible—at least that is what we believe. So, as you see, the financial life cycle tracks the human life

23

cycle. As our physical life is extended, our financial life cycle and its components change in tandem.

It is to this end I am dedicated to seeing a family think in terms of evolving a personal financial formula which will enable each family member to "smell the roses" as they go along. They should enjoy feelings of adequate preparation for the latter stages of the financial cycle during the earlier stages without sacrificing a comfortable lifestyle, a certainly honorable and intelligent goal for all of us to pursue.

As we begin to explore the six elements of personal finance in more detail, i.e., liquidity and cash flow, insurance, public and private benefits, credit, investments and estate planning I strongly urge you to reflect on the approximate period of the Financial Life Cycle in which you presently find yourself. If you will look back from your present situation you will discern feelings you had during those earlier periods. This will help you to better anticipate feelings you'll likely have in the future. Reflections and anticipations enable you to do a better job of relating to the current personal financial picture as it pertains to your individual up-to-date situation. In all of these periods of the Financial Life Cycle a balanced financial life is desirable and in order. That is to say, a wise selection and use of credit, picking proper investments, owning the right insurance, building benefits, sound estate planning and making proper provisions for adequate cash flow and liquidity in a balanced form provide the desired results for you and your loved ones throughout your financial life cycle.

Instead of stuffing cash into sofas and hiding your assets in old boxes, enjoy your wealth—regardless of how little or how much you have. Shove any feelings of guilt out of your mind and get set to advance to Sound Financial Planning—the next chapter.

Chapter Three

SOUND FINANCIAL PLANNING

To achieve the greatest financial peace of mind and the rewards which normally accompany a peaceful mind, we must develop a basic personal financial program and follow the program while updating and fine-tuning it along the way. The following are extremely important considerations as we initiate the thinking and planning stages.

Moreism. "Moreism" will not be a valid premise for the future. We should not base our financial futures simply on the premise that there will *always* be *more* of everything on an annual basis—more income and more assets—more of anything or everything, thanks to inflation. Rather we must think in terms of productivity and apply our own wisdom and experience. Confidence in our ability to define and use incomes and resources becomes an important element in our planning process. These factors constitute valuable predictable functions for our sound financial plan.

We should also understand our own motivators. Are we existing in a personal hope-for-gain or a fear-of-loss mode? Priorities are extremely important.

Priorities. First of all we must be certain we have the ability to accomplish what we desire in life. We must provide for our needs: food, clothing, shelter, transportation and health. The *second* priority is to use modern financial and legal tools available to us to deal with the contingencies of life: living too long, dying too soon or experiencing a form of life-debilitating illness or accident. *Third,* we must be certain we are wisely planning for the satisfaction of responsibilities which have been assumed or have been thrust upon us: educating the children and assisting handicapped or disabled members of the family. Don't overlook obligations to elderly family members. *Fourth,* we must evolve a strategy to determine and accommodate an appropriate amount of consumption versus savings. We should be certain we are making maximum use of our employer, private and public benefit programs. *Fifth,* build an adequate cash reserve. And *sixth,* decide what percentage of income is to be saved or invested versus the amount spent each year.

Each of these six priority factors will be additionally considered in subsequent chapters. There will be a great deal more about these important subjects as we proceed through the financial cycle. After we make these priority determinations and decisions we will get on with the business of living and enjoying our lives. We can live our lives without a feeling of guilt or neglecting others, as well as provide for ourselves adequately, and develop a sense of truly being able to afford to live as we are living. Or, let's say, living as we would like to.

With these facts in mind, we should recognize where we are in the financial life cycle. What is the potential impact of inheritance or family dependence? What are our goals? What is it we *really* seek? We must continue to be aware of both our changing society and our own motivational changes as we move through life.

Key Elements of Sound Financial Planning

There are several key factors in financial planning to which everyone must address time and attention. (Chart 3.1) First, understand what you have. Be certain you develop a personal financial statement and a realistic cash-flow plan. Second, define, communicate and commit to the accomplishment of your goals. Be certain the family members, particularly husband and wife, are working and striving *together* in terms of what they want to accomplish each year and over the entire financial life cycle.

Third, develop a personal financial strategy. Most of us deal with day-to-day financial obstacles yet seldom develop a carefully thought out financial strategy to accomplish our goals. By obstacles I mean, as an example, we acquire insurance as we move through life but seldom change it. As a rule, we don't even *review* the policies on a periodic schedule. Similarly, we dabble in various investments and find we are better buyers than sellers. Once a will is made we tend to feel that it is adequate forevermore and do not review it and change it as our personal and financial lives evolve. So a personal financial strategy is extremely important if we are to reach our goals. A financial plan

Key Elements Of Sound Financial Planning

- Understand What You Have

- Define Your Goals

- Develop A Personal Financial Strategy

- Develop and Maintain Personal Financial Discipline

CHART 3.1

is like a flowing river. It constantly changes whether we do anything about it or not.

Fourth, we need to develop and maintain the personal and financial discipline necessary to accomplish our financial goals. Like physical fitness, it is extremely difficult to maintain good exercise programs without the discipline to be certain the programs are reviewed and updated on a regular basis. Otherwise, we may fail to achieve our objectives in our physical and fiscal lives. Once we have taken inventory, have defined our goals and developed a strategy to accomplish those objectives, it is encumbent upon us to be certain we develop and maintain the personal financial discipline to carry out our strategies and reach our goals. Some people tend to merely watch the river flow by. Others are thinking in terms of how the power of the flow can be used, how to benefit from the tides, how to use the river to reach an objective.

There are several basic preparations we should make in defining what we have. First is the preparation and maintenance of a current personal financial statement. (Chart 3.2) Your balance sheet should list all of your assets and all of your liabilities and compute your net worth. This should be accomplished at least on an annual basis. Be sure to include your employer benefit plans, that is, the portion of your plans which are partially or fully vested. If you should decide to leave or if you are terminated from your current employment, what are your rights? At what date do you become fully vested? What about early retirement benefits? Do you know the answers?

Also prepare, on an annual basis, a personal cash-flow statement in which you determine not only the amount of cash available to you from your salary, bonus, investments, as well as a sale of assets, but also a clear estimate of federal, state and local taxes. (Chart 3.3)

Personal Net Worth Statement

Assets

Cash	$ _____
Stocks & Bonds	_____
Notes Receivable	_____
Cash Value of Insurance	_____
Automobiles	_____
Real Estate	
Home	_____
Vacation Home	_____
Commercial	_____
Company Benefits	
Thrift/401K Plan	_____
Stock Option Bargain Element	_____
Retirement Benefit	_____
Personal Property	_____
Household Furnishings	_____
Other Assets	_____
Total Assets	**$ $ $**

Liabilities

Notes Payable	$ _____
Taxes Due	_____
Insurance Loans	_____
Due on Automobiles	_____
Due on Real Estate	
Home	_____
Vacation Home	_____
Commercial	_____
Other Liabilities	_____
Total Liabilities	**$ $**
Net Worth	$ _____

CHART 3.2

Personal Cash Flow Statement

Income

Salary	$ _____			
Bonus	_____			
Investments	_____			
Other	_____	$ _____		

Less: Estimated

Federal Income Tax	$ _____		
State Income Tax	_____		
Social Security	_____		
Payroll Deductions	_____		
Other	_____	(_____)	

Disposable Income $

Less: Expenditures

Mortgage Payments	$ _____		
Investment Debt	_____		
Consumer Debt	_____		
Insurance Premiums	_____		
Personal Living Expenses	_____		
Tuition/Support	_____		
Savings	_____		
Other	_____	(_____)	

Net Cash Flow $ _____

CHART 3.3

Goal Setting and Financial Considerations

Appropriate considerations relating to defining goals include the following (Chart 3.4): First, resist peer pressure and avoid group decision-making schemes. We are more diverse as human beings today than we think we are. It was suitable for the farmers in an agrarian society of several decades ago to meet on a Saturday, sit around the potbellied stove in the small country town and swap tales and exchange ideas. The common location of farms in a relatively similar environment with like soil conditions and related family situations provided a stage for worthwhile ideas back in the "good old" days of rural America. This is not necessarily true in today's complex, urbanized and specialized vocational society. My experience indicates that two vice-presidents in identical positions of the same company, both with the same stock options, same cost basis in the stock, same incomes and even like ages, have vastly differing financial needs and economic requirements. These differences may afford one an opportunity to exercise his stock options, using credit to accomplish the transaction. The other executive may not be able to afford to exercise his options due to cash-flow requirements caused by family circumstances, different goals and lifestyles. One executive might have two elderly parents in a nursing home causing a substantial cash-flow drain. The other may have received an inheritance of a half-million dollars. So it is difficult and even hazardous for one to advise another or for an individual to follow the actions or reactions of another. Odds are we would not accomplish the same financial objectives even if one followed another's plan, even under what would appear to be similar circumstances.

Second, what are the needs of you and your family members? Consider the size of the home, education requirements and the health factors of each member of the family.

Third, what are your lifestyle choices? Would you like to own a second home? A houseboat? Your own airplane? What are the requirements of the family for travel and other large-expense lifestyle choices? How about a trip around the world? A tour of old Mexico?

Fourth, what is your attitude toward investments? How much risk can you tolerate? Can you stand to be in debt? Do you want to owe money? What are your accumulation objectives? Be honest with yourself in evaluating each one of these attitudes. People have diverse feelings with respect to debt, for example. Some people feel their income and assets *should* be leveraged to produce greater accumulation objectives. Others simply cannot emotionally cope with owing money to anyone for any reason. Each of us has our own particular risk barometer. Through the help of a competent financial counsellor you will be able to avoid substantial problems attendant to the elements of debt and risk. A qualified counsellor should be able to show you how debt is used constructively.

Fifth, what are your long-term objectives? Your *real* longer-term objectives? Do you want to retire? Or at what would be a normal retirement

Considerations Related To Defining Goals

- **Resist Peer Pressure And Avoid Group Decision Making**

- **Needs Of Family Members**
  - Size Of Home
  - Education
  - Health

- **Lifestyle Choices**
  - Vacation Home
  - Other

- **Attitude Toward Investments**
  - Tolerance Of Debt And Risk
  - Accumulation Objectives

- **Longer-Term Objectives**
  - Retirement
  - Estate Disposition

CHART 3.4

time do you want to enter another vocation requiring income or the investment of capital? Your longer-term objective will vary depending on your answers to these questions. What are your estate disposition objectives? Do you wish to provide a large estate for your children or other members of your family? Are you charitably inclined? Or do you, as many people indicate, simply wish to spend that which has been accumulated?

Personal financial strategy. Having defined your goals and understanding better what you have and where your cash is coming from and going to, you are now in the enviable position of being able to create a personal financial strategy. (Chart 3.5) The key factors for your strategy development are that you have (1) financial exposure or benefits due to family requirements or anticipated inheritances, (2) a clear definition and program for accomplishing your accumulation objectives, and (3) a development of this strategy into a three-tiered evaluation. *First,* does the strategy you have adopted make personal sense? Is it something you can cope with in terms of risk assumption, debt involvement and personal current situations? *Second,* does the strategy make economic sense? Is it a strategy that will produce satisfactory economic results in a safe fashion considering all of the vicissitudes and risks involved? And *third,* does the strategy accommodate maximum tax advantages or results? My experience indicates that all financial strategies should be developed in this fashion and using these factors and steps. Does it make personal sense? Does it make economic and tax sense? But always in that order. Serious dislocations or poor results occur when the proper sequence is violated. Putting tax considerations ahead of personal and economic, for example, is courting disaster in your plan.

(4) Ask yourself: where am I and where is my family in the Financial Life Cycle? Are we in the accumulation phases or the preservation phases? And what has happened to us so far in our financial life which will have an economic impact on our futures, and in our particular situation? (5) As we evolve our financial strategy we should be maintaining our vocation-to-investment-income ratio so that we can at all times determine whether we are making satisfactory progress towards substituting passive income and pensions for active vocational, professional or business income productivity. (6) And we should, in evolving our financial strategy, be constantly making a determination as to whether we should be *concentrating* or *diversifying* to reach our stated financial objectives. We should concentrate on accumulating that which we know something about. We should seek investment media we are familiar with and feel comfortable in accumulating; then later we can diversify. Seek out investments that will protect value now and which will provide income later.

Financial planning is a dynamic on-going process. Like our day-to-day circumstances which change from one object to another, financial planning is always subject to change as circumstances dictate. It is a process you shouldn't

Personal Financial Strategy

- Inheritance Or Financial Exposure

- Accumulation Objectives

- (1) Personal, (2) Economic, (3) Tax

- Financial Life Cycle

- Vocational To Investment Income Sheet

- Concentration Or Diversification

CHART 3.5

34

attempt alone and no one can do totally for you. It's not a "quick fix" and not a project to be completed over a weekend. It's a team-work project requiring objectivity and outside expertise, plus time. It does, however, involve your thinking through those things which you must be aware of and prudently analyzing what you want to accomplish in your life. Your plan will usually be for yourself. It affects others while you're alive and will even provide for those who remain after your death. Personal financial planning is personal. However, with help from a qualified financial counsellor, you can remove a great deal of fear and uncertainty from the decision-making process. A qualified counsellor adds dimension and perspective to the plan process. It is usually fear and confusion which cause us to *procrastinate* and to ultimately make bad investment decisions or simply do nothing at all. It's scary to realize how easy it is to avoid sensible estate planning, to do a poor job of cash-flow analysis, to overlook budgeting, and to make bad investment decisions. Most clients tell me they spend *more* time and energy *avoiding* planning than they used in completing their personal financial plan. Others, it seems, are focusing on the incorrect elements.

For example, a major shortcoming in many financial plans is inadequate disability income provisions. Most people pay attention more to what would happen to the family financial requirements and needs in the event of death than to family needs during periods of total or partial disability. I refer to this as the "living death" because the breadwinner is *dead* as a provider but remains alive as a consumer.

One of the more dramatic demonstrations of *living death* occurred recently. An executive in his mid–50's had, due to his company's benefit programs, come to depend too greatly on the provisions of the company-sponsored disability program. The disability provision of his employer's plan provided for disability payments amounting to approximately 15% of his salary. Unfortunately, this man suffered a massive stroke before taking action on our advice to increase his disability protection through a private contract. We had suggested he increase coverage to at least 60% of his salary. The reason for 60% is to replace take-home pay rather than attempt to insure his gross income. Disability income insurance can be bought with *after*-tax dollars rather than pre-tax dollars. Therefore, benefits are not taxed when received by the insured. The executive had three teenaged children, one in college, one within two years of beginning college, the other much younger. He was married to a former citizen of a European country who knew absolutely nothing of U.S. investments or benefit programs. As a matter of fact, she didn't even know how to drive a car. Upon total disability, the income stream from the executive's employer dropped to 15% of what it had been. Medical expenses, though covered by an excellent medical program, put an additional burden on the family's cash-flow requirements. The wife had to find employment. The combination of the employer-sponsored plan, disability provisions under Social Security and the wife's income were grossly inadequate to meet the income needs of the family. The home had to be sold to make provision for investment capital in order to produce supplemental income. In short, a complete lifestyle reversal and rearrangement were the uncomfortable bottom line. While none would like to admit it, the unpleasant truth is the family would have been better off financially if he had been killed by the stroke.

By realistically taking inventory of what you have, by defining and maintaining a surveillance program for your personal goals, by evolving a financial strategy to accomplish those goals, and by defining and establishing a system for personal discipline to be certain your strategy is executed on a timely basis, you will enjoy a satisfying financial existence and have greater peace of mind in all of your undertakings, both personal and professional. Sound financial planning improves *all aspects of living.* Don't think of a financial plan as being involved only with monetary matters. If the disabled executive had planned for his disability, he and his family would have enjoyed *all aspects of living.* I have known cases where an individual's total personality changed—for the better, I must add—after he faced up to the realities of his financial life and future, and after he did something about it!!

THE WIDOW'S MITE

"I wish I had known . . ." a string of simple words financial counsellors hear much too often. I again heard these words a dozen times from the widow of a recently deceased acquaintance. Her husband died at the young age of 47 years. The man's will was twenty years old and had been prepared at the time the young couple resided in another state—a state which, by the way, has entirely different probate laws from those in Texas, the home state when he expired. Unfortunately, the wife knew next to nothing about her husband's corporate benefits. She had only a sketchy knowledge of the family's assets, liabilities and insurance. His untimely death and the lack of family planning meant one lifetime exemption was lost. The harried widow was forced into quickly making crucial decisions involving several hundred thousand dollars. Who can be expected to make consistently correct choices under such circumstances? Each time I counseled with her, she must have said, "I wish I'd known about . . ." at least ten times and probably on more than twenty occasions. She wished she had been enlightened about the husband's benefits. She regretted that she was unaware of the importance of reviewing a will when moving from one state to another. She wished she had known about estate taxes, legal tax exemptions and probate laws. At one point she turned to me with tear-filled eyes and told me that she *should have known* her husband was a candidate for a heart attack. She explained that her husband's father and brother had both died at an early age of cardiovascular problems. "I knew that heart trouble is hereditary, and I knew the odds weren't in Harold's favor . . . but I didn't want to think about him dying first," she whispered. After a pause, she added, "There's so much I *should have known.*" And to think that her late husband was a highly paid advisor who spent his working years solving major problems for his clients!

But death is not the only time when people talk about what they wish they had known. Some people have paid for costly educations for their children with after-tax dollars because they didn't know better. Some have provided assistance for elderly parents and have made gifts to children and grandchildren with after-income-taxed funds instead of using appreciated assets. Unfortunately, some business owners sell a business or a tract of land or other assets before getting financial counselling. When they later learn of the amount of taxes that *could have been* saved had the transaction been structured differently, the counsellor knows almost verbatim what will be said next: "I wish I'd known about that."

In meetings with women's groups the most prevalent complaint I hear is that they were totally unaware of their family's financial situation. Their husbands were not communicating with them; they did not know where they stood or what they had. They did not know what decisions would be facing them at a time they would be least prepared to cope with those decisions. It appears there's a growing resentment within the marital relationships because of this lack of knowledge and communication. Could it be there is a relationship between the lack of financial communication and our modern-day divorce rates? Some day we may come to recognize that the family that plans together stays together.

Chapter Four

STAYING AFLOAT: MANAGING YOUR CASH FLOW AND STAYING LIQUID

Since most people obviously do not like to think in terms of living on a budget, I have, therefore, elected to identify the budgeting process as "cash-flow management." In economic lives, regardless of what stage of the life cycle we may find ourselves in, we must develop a personal financial strategy for the management of cash which comes into our possession. It doesn't matter whether the cash comes to us on a regular or irregular basis, what's paramount is that it *must be properly managed.* This is called a ***cash management system*** as indicated on Chart 4.1.

You must first develop a master distribution account into which you conceptualize salary, bonus, investment income and other cash gains flowing. Next make provision for an evaluation of your fixed expenses such as mortgage payments, debt service and insurance premiums. Those things, given your present lifestyle and obligations, usually remain relatively fixed throughout any given twelve-month period. Then calculate and provide for all of your variable expenses—"running around money" is what I prefer to call these expenses. (Chart 4.2) There are disbursements which can vary somewhat depending upon cash available or one's lifestyle indulgences. Nevertheless, they become important factors when considering overall cash requirement and allocations. All sound plans have "running around" types of flexibility. If more people could recognize this feature of financial planning, the idea of budgets would not be such an obstacle for them.

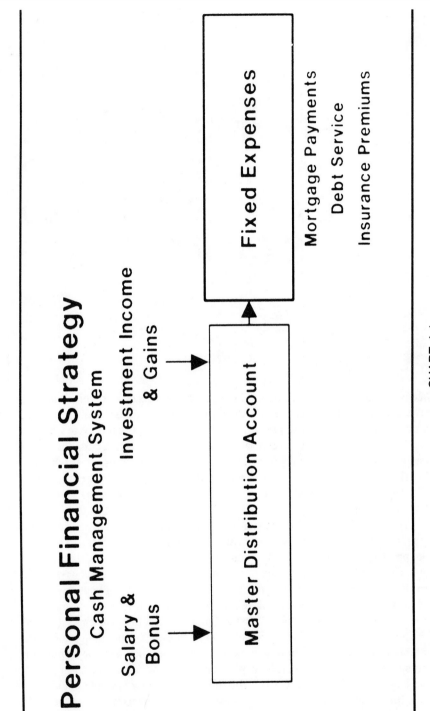

Personal Financial Strategy
Cash Management System

Salary & Bonus

Investment Income & Gains

Master Distribution Account

Fixed Expenses

Mortgage Payments

Debt Service

Insurance Premiums

CHART 4.1

40

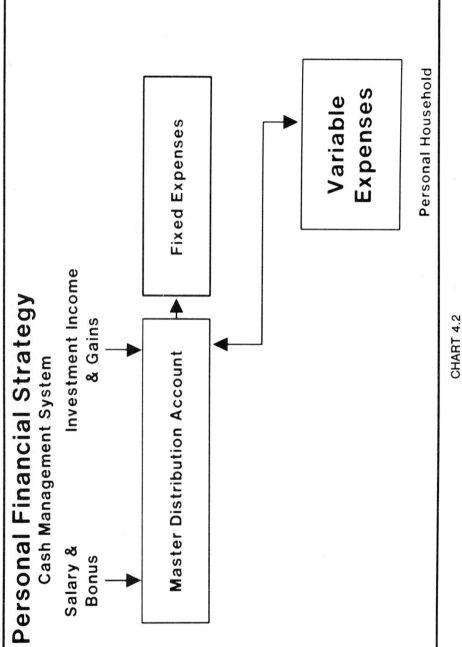

Personal Financial Strategy
Cash Management System

Salary & Bonus

Investment Income & Gains

Master Distribution Account

Fixed Expenses

Variable Expenses

Personal Household

CHART 4.2

41

Most of my clients, before we started advising them, were not making adequate provision for what I call lifestyle depreciation, i.e., provision for household appliances and home repairs or replacement and automobile repairs or replacement. (Chart 4.3) Allowing provisions for vacation requirements is also extremely important. Yet so many overlook these aspects in their financial planning. Adequate allowance should be made for monthly as well as annual cash-flow amounts into their *depreciation accruals.*

IMPORTANT POINTS: Budgets are not limited to money spent but also involve non-cash items like depreciation. Financial planning does not concern itself with only monetary matters.

Provision for adequate liquid reserves is an essential step that must be developed in every plan. Liquidity means sufficient cash reserves in the form of money market funds, certificates of deposits or treasury bills to provide a "sinking" fund for emergencies and for carrying investments through periods of higher-than-anticipated interest rates, and/or slower-than-contemplated investment returns. Changes in the economic environment, unanticipated fluctuations in prices of the investment are two more reasons for this type of sinking fund. Call it a "staying power" reserve providing ability to stay with an investment or with a commitment even though it may not evolve as anticipated. This form of contingency planning is critical to the ultimate success of every financial plan. If an investor has all of his cash flow and credit tied up and is without adequate liquid reserves, he may be forced to sell an investment to reduce a loan or be required to pay higher interest rates in negative market conditions. Sound planning means never being forced into a financial corner. While our initial commitment and our use of credit for whatever investment media selected may have been wisely chosen, timing may preclude us from consummating the commitment according to the plan. This can occur because we failed to have adequate liquidity to maintain the investment through unanticipated situations, unless, of course, we have a sinking fund included in the overall plan. Hence the need for the personal liquidity reserve—it can make the difference between loss and gain in key aspects of the total program. (Chart 4.4)

Next we should create an adequate tax reserve. (Chart 4.5) It is not necessary that we arrange for withholding or quarterly installments to be totally adequate to meet our anticipated income tax requirements. Rather we can keep certain amounts of anticipated taxes which are not necessary to meet required withholding or quarterly installments invested to provide additional income. A wise planner should be able to reasonably estimate taxes at the beginning of each year rather than wait for the return to be prepared on April 15 of the following year. This unnecessary postponement can result in the need to liquidate assets or borrow money to pay additional taxes—both of which may prove to be in adverse economic conditions of high interest rates or during poor market conditions. Either way, the taxpayer could suffer loss—a loss which could have been avoided through planning. Instead, you should estimate your

Personal Financial Strategy
Cash Management System

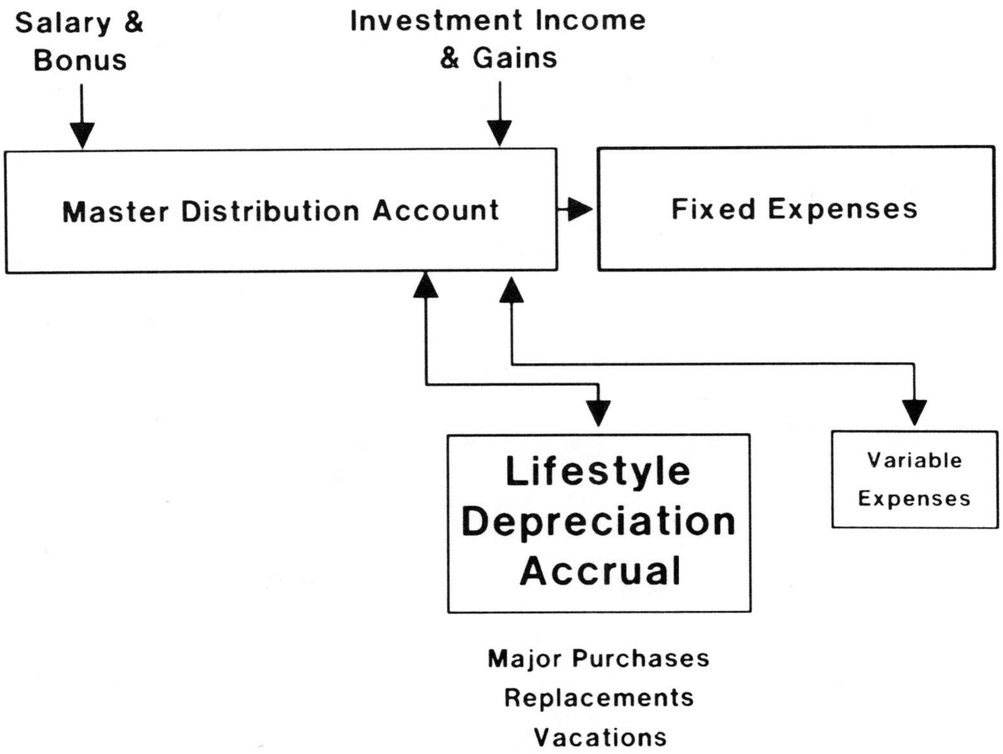

Salary & Bonus

Investment Income & Gains

Master Distribution Account

Fixed Expenses

Variable Expenses

Lifestyle Depreciation Accrual

Major Purchases
Replacements
Vacations

CHART 4.3

43

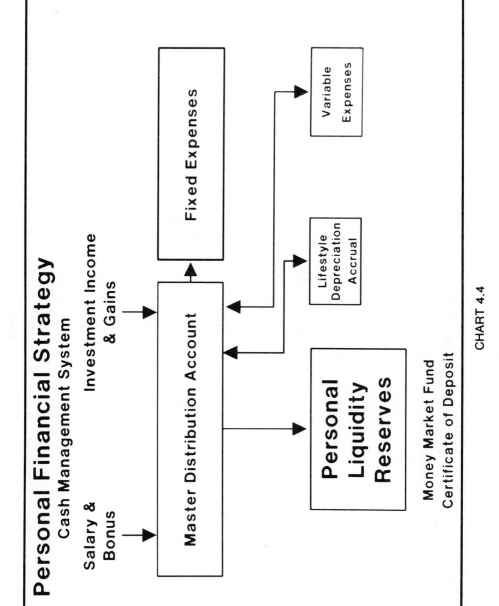

Personal Financial Strategy
Cash Management System

Salary & Bonus

Investment Income & Gains

Master Distribution Account

Fixed Expenses

Variable Expenses

Lifestyle Depreciation Accrual

Personal Liquidity Reserves

Money Market Fund
Certificate of Deposit

CHART 4.4

44

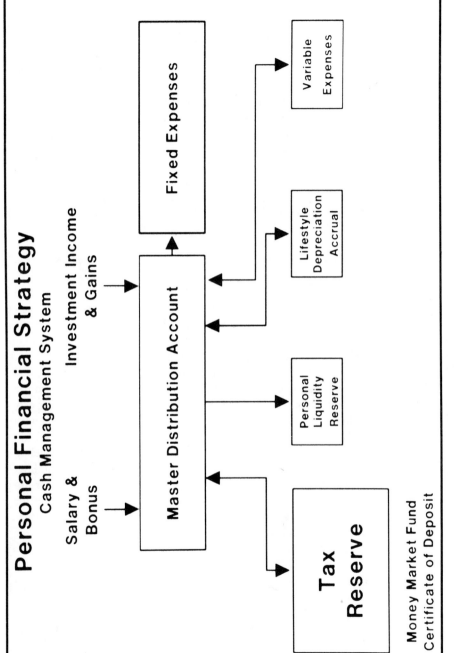

Personal Financial Strategy
Cash Management System

Salary & Bonus

Investment Income & Gains

Master Distribution Account

Fixed Expenses

Variable Expenses

Lifestyle Depreciation Accrual

Personal Liquidity Reserve

Tax Reserve

Money Market Fund
Certificate of Deposit

CHART 4.5

tax requirements going into the year and make adequate provisions for reserves over and above withholding or quarterly installments. This way cash is available to meet anticipated additional amounts due when the tax return itself, and the tax, is due. Sound planning equals no surprises.

By investing the reserve in CDs or money market funds, added income is realized while costly penalties are avoided. The astute planner is a two-time winner, not a double loser.

Having made provisions in your master distribution account for adequate amounts of fixed and variable expenses and for depreciation reserves, personal liquidity and taxes, you are now in a position to contemplate the amounts to be devoted to investments, but only after *all* of these cash requirement situations have been satisfied. (Chart 4.6) Your first consideration in determining your investment provisions is the amounts to be contributed to your private and employer benefit programs. Take maximum advantage of these programs. They are tax-favored and provide a multitude of advantages to the well-planned taxpayer. Your individual retirement account and/or Keogh plan can be one of your most profitable investments. Consider how much cash you can contribute to your employer benefit programs. These investment opportunities include thrift savings plans, pension programs, salary deferral programs, stock option and stock purchase programs and deferred compensation arrangements. After taking maximum advantage of tax-advantaged investment opportunities, you are then in a position to determine how much of your cash flow and assets you have available for other investments. These may include stocks, bonds, real estate, oil and gas activities or other media.

If you will manage your cash flow as opposed to letting cash flow become a reactive knee jerk, you will discover you will be able to make maximum use of cash in accomplishing your personal financial strategy. Failure to properly and efficiently manage cash causes serious financial displacements along with uncomfortable financial problems. Communications relating to cash within the family are often difficult or confusing. For example, if the husband is feeling this is the year to buy a new car while, at the same time, the wife is thinking in terms of taking an extended vacation, they quickly realize that neither objective can be satisfied because the "money isn't there." Wise planning for cash management can enable both objectives to be accomplished without neglecting other financial requirements.

While many financial planning conflicts appear to be unconquerable mountains, I have learned that through communications, planning and good old fashioned reasoning some obstacles turn out to be mere molehills. A recent occurrence supports this premise.

My clients, a Houston couple, had encountered the previously-mentioned car/vacation obstacle. The husband wanted a new car while the wife felt equally strong that what the couple needed more was a long, relaxing vacation. During a financial planning session in my office the two opinions surfaced. After a period of listening to each voice their feelings, I suggested that both were correct. They indeed needed a new car *and* a luxurious vaca-

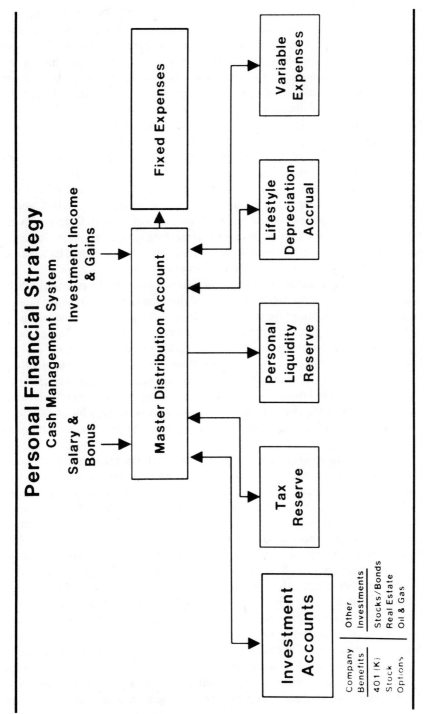

Personal Financial Strategy
Cash Management System

Salary & Bonus

Investment Income & Gains

Master Distribution Account

Fixed Expenses

Variable Expenses

Lifestyle Depreciation Accrual

Personal Liquidity Reserve

Tax Reserve

Investment Accounts

Company Benefits	Other Investments
401 (K)	Stocks/Bonds
Stock Options	Real Estate
	Oil & Gas

CHART 4.6

tion! Fortunately for all concerned at the time the U.S. dollar was extremely strong in relation to other currencies. The German mark was no exception. Why not travel to Germany, purchase a German-made vehicle and bring the car back to the States? The amount of money to be saved by purchasing the car at the factory in Germany, not to mention having the use of the car for touring Europe, would more than pay the cost of the trip. Not only did the couple follow this advice, but I later learned they returned a year later for a repeat performance. This time the car they purchased in Europe was resold in the States for a tidy profit. Some clients are extremely fast learners.

Unfortunately not all family financial conflicts are so easily resolved. Solomon-like advice doesn't always satisfy both parties. Circumstances are not always as ideal as in this particular case. I really don't know what my advice would have been in the automobile/vacation matter had the U.S. dollar been weak in comparison to the mark. However, I continue to believe with all my heart that there's no substitute for maintaining strong open lines for communications, especially in financial matters. An attitude of "Come, let's reason together" makes a lot of sense when it comes to dollars.

Chart 4.7 illustrates a cash-flow analysis which should be prepared yearly in advance. This enables you to determine what you are spending your money on and where it's coming from. It also aids in making intelligent decisions as to whether or not you are satisfied with the way the money is being spent. Corrections must be made for the successful planner to accomplish the desired financial requirements of the family in a simple and satisfactory manner. Often it's not how much you spend; it's whether or not you are spending the funds in a mutually desired direction and producing results in the form of enjoyable family financial living. Remember these three important keys for satisfactory family financial planning: communications, communications, communications.

In the long run all expenses are variable. Little or nothing in a financial plan is etched in marble. You will find existing debt service commitments, present home overhead, allowances for children and other family dependents, plus other expenses, are relatively fixed. However, you must know exactly what those items add up to in order to determine how much you may allow out of your discretionary income for other expense factors. (Chart 4.8) After you take the variable expenses from your discretionary income you will be able to determine your net cash flow, or deficit, as the case may be. (Chart 4.9) You should know, of course, that in some years your net cash flow will likely be negative. This happens when you have paid off substantial debt or incurred unusual nonrecurring expenses for home appliances or furnishings, automobiles and/or a second home or a recreational vehicle. Don't let this worry you. A negative cash flow is not necessarily a problem in the family's personal financial picture—only if it is sustained over a period of years or becomes an annual habit. The important thing is that you know what your net cash flow is each year and whether it is a positive or negative. The cautious planner

Cash Flow Analysis

Income	Monthly	Annually
Salary (Net of W/H)		
Bonus		
Dividends & Interest		
Other (Gifts, Tax Refund)		
Total Income		

Fixed Expenses	Monthly	Annually
Taxes (Over Payroll Deductions)		
Food		
Housing		
Transportation		
Insurance		
Other, Etc.		
Total Fixed Expenses		

CHART 4.7

Cash Flow Analysis

Discretionary Income	Monthly	Annually
Total Income		
Less: (Fixed Expenses)	( )	( )
Total Discretionary Income		

CHART 4.8

Cash Flow Analysis

Variable Expenses	Monthly	Annually
Clothing		
Vacations & Recreation		
Gifts		
Personal Allowances		
Other		
Total Variable Expenses		

Cash Flow	Monthly	Annually
Discretionary Income Less: (Variable Expenses)	( )	( )
Net Cash Flow (Deficits)		

CHART 4.9

knows he or she has a program for accommodating or overcoming the excess or deficit through the financial plan. Sound planning accommodates the "unexpected" times of deficit spending and negative cash flow. Pity the poor soul who encounters these "financial problems" without a long-term intelligent plan. No wonder people who plan seem to enjoy better health and maintain a more positive outlook on life than non-planners. (Chart 4.10)

Chart 4.11 illustrates the importance of depreciation reserves. It shows the monthly funding needed to replace a $12,000 automobile every four years, to provide for an annual vacation expenditure of $6,000, and to provide for an estimated average cost of repairs and maintenance at the household level. The total for these three items, in the most simple of family depreciation reserve estimates, indicates a monthly accrual of $900. The depreciation accrual is to be transferred from your NOW or checking account monthly to a savings vehicle. Money market funds work well for this purpose. Your expenditures for replacement of automobile, a vacation or home maintenance should, of course, be spent from the accrual account and not from your regular NOW or checking account. After a period of time you will have an adequate evaluation of whether you are accruing too much or not enough for these depreciation items.

It has been my experience that most people, in the earlier stages of the life cycle when income is lower, are inclined to accept my advice for providing an orderly accumulation for funds or replacement of durable assets and maintenance more often than older people with higher incomes. This is also true of those with fixed incomes. The fact that these are typical patterns does not lessen their desirability for all persons interested in sound financial planning providing for depreciation at the household level. This is particularly true during the survival period of the life cycle when cash flow is a predominant concern in most households. This is usually when children are in their teenage years and the typical family is living in a large home with higher maintenance requirements. Sometimes a second home is purchased along with a boat or recreational vehicle, each requiring extra maintenance and replacement costs. Vacation expenses are usually higher at this stage of the financial cycle. Ironically, many people who need a depreciation reserve the most are the ones without one.

The magic of the depreciation reserve was made crystal clear to me in years past when many banks and savings institutions offered so-called vacation and Christmas savings plans. It never ceased to amaze me that so many people availed themselves of these no-interest programs. I often puzzled over this phenomenon. The answer, of course, is that these *un-economic* savings plans were in fact a system for creating depreciation-like reserves in advance of need. When vacation or Christmas time came, the savers were able to pay for their vacation and Christmas expenditures without invading other funds or the month-to-month cash flow. This simplistic plan added a valuable and useful plus to the family's financial picture. The more I thought about them, the

Basic Liquidity Categories

I. Lifestyle Costs

- Average Monthly Personal and Living Expenses

- Checking or N.O.W. Accounts

II. Depreciation Reserve

- Estimated Costs of Maintaining or Replacing True Depreciating Assets Related to Lifestyle (Home Autos, Boats, Major Household Goods)

- Interest Bearing Liquidity Fund

III. Liquid Reserves

- Emergency, Opportunity, Investment Defense, "Feel Good" Money, "Sinking Fund"

- One-Year Maturity (Or Less) Liquidable Market Instruments

CHART 4.10

53

Depreciation Reserve Estimates

	Monthly Funding
Automobile (1)	
Target: 12,000 (Adjusted for Trade Salvage and Price Increase)	250
Accrual Period: 4 Years	
Vacation Accrual	
Target: 6,000	500
Accrual Period: Annual	
Household Maintenance	
Empirical or Estimated Average Target (Painting, A.C., Appliances, Etc.,: Age Factors)	150
	900

CHART 4.11

more I have come to appreciate the rationale behind these no-interest savings plans. Bankers think of them as gimmicks to attract low-cost deposits. The customer looks on them as a systematic method of creating reserves for a predicted need. Voila! A win/win proposition and a useful financial planning tool.

You can improve your cash flow substantially by contributing appreciated assets to satisfy charitable requirements on an annual basis. If you give appreciated stock in lieu of cash as is illustrated in Chart 4.12 you will effect an overall tax savings.

This form of cash-flow enhancement has numerous advantages. If the donor desires to retain ownership of a particular stock in which there is a low cost base, the giver may make a charitable gift of the stock and use the cash he would have given the charity to repurchase the stock at current market value. The donor thereby increases the cost basis in the stock value without incurring capital gain tax liabilities. The donor reduces capital gain taxes when later selling the stock. Assuming the stock continues to grow in value, this method of "giving" securities may be repeated again and again over a period of years.

We also recommend this procedure as a method for diversifying a client's concentration in a single stock. Rather than recommending the client sell the stock and incur a capital gain, we suggest he use the stock, in lieu of cash, for charitable contributions, thus gradually reducing the concentration in the one stock using cash that otherwise would have been given to charity for alternate diversified investments.

Clifford Trusts

An interesting way to accommodate cash-flow requirements for educating children or to assist elderly dependent parents is accomplished through the use of a Clifford Trust. By placing income-producing assets in a trust, known as either a Clifford Trust or a reversionary or short-term trust, income from the assets may be paid to the recipient (object of the trust: the beneficiary) as opposed to the grantor (creator) of the trust. A trust of this type must last for at least 10 years and one day, or for the life of the grantor or for the life of the beneficiary(s), whichever is shorter. Through such an arrangement the income tax burden is transferred from the parents, for example, to the children. The youngsters are likely to be in a much lower tax bracket than the parents. This action reduces, in effect, the cost of education or support of dependents. Income, of course, cannot be transferred in this matter to satisfy normal parental obligations but can be used for contributions such as private schooling, college education and gifts which are not parental obligations.

There are at least two practical ways to fund a Clifford Trust. For example, a client recently placed into a Clifford Trust $100,000 worth of a particular stock which he intended to keep indefinitely. The shares were given to the trust; however, they later reverted back to the donor. The stock paid a

Charitable Gift Illustration

	Case I Gift Cash and Invest After Tax Proceeds of Stock Sold	Case II Gift Stock and Utilize Cash on Hand to Invest
Amount Given to Charity	$1,000 Cash	$1,000 FMV Stock
Tax Savings In a 50% Tax Bracket	$ 500	$ 500
Investable Funds: FMV Stock Sold Less: Capital Gains Tax	$1,000 (200)	
Net Investable Funds	$ 800	$1,000 Cash
Total Cash In Hand From Investable Funds and Charitable Gift Tax Savings	$1,300	$1,500
Net Savings From Gifting Stock as Opposed to Gifting Cash	$200	

CHART 4.12

yearly dividend of 9% or $9,000. Before transfer to the trust the $9,000 income had been largely lost due to taxation at the donor's high tax bracket. (Chart 4.13) In the Clifford Trust the $9,000 yearly dividend, distributed as income for educational purposes for the children, was more productively used. The dividend was for the most part not taxed due to the fact that the children had no other income. In this instance, an asset was used to fund the trust, an asset which was to be *retained* by the family. In the meantime, for ten years, the stock provided income for college expenses while the incidence of tax on the dividends was substantially reduced.

A second method for funding a Clifford Trust is to use the credit of the parent to borrow cash for funding the trust. The assets (cash) in the trust may be invested in income-producing properties (real estate, stocks, bonds, etc.) to provide income to the children. The interest payable to the bank becomes a tax deduction in the parents' cash flow.

Chart 4.14 reflects the cash-flow comparisons considering alternates for funding educational expenses and for funding a salary deferral program. You will note in all illustrations the client's base salary is established at $120,000 a year. In this situation, while paying his children's tuition and contributing to a thrift savings plan with after-tax dollars, the family enjoys a net cash flow of $20,061. (Chart 4.15) Using the Clifford Trust as illustrated, by borrowing $110,000 and amortizing the repayment of the loan over the 10-year life of the trust, the client provides $11,000 for the children's education and the trustee's fee and tax, while enjoying an improved cash flow from $20,061 to $21,859! (Charts 4.16 and 4.17) The $1,798 a year difference represents added spendable cash. The salary deferral plan enabling the client to contribute pre-tax rather than after-tax dollars to his salary deferral (401K) program and continue the after-tax payment of tuition of $9,000 means the client's cash flow remains the same. This is true even though the client contributed *twice* the amount to his employer's savings plan: from $4,000 to $8,000. Combining the two, the client's cash flow is improved by $1,723 a year, while saving $110,000 due to the amortization of the bank loan. The net improvement comes to approximately $150 a month in cash available for the parents.

There are other satisfactory and attractive accumulation objectives which may be accomplished through the use of the Clifford Trust. By borrowing the funds to be placed in the trust and forcing a lifetime accumulation participation by the parent, the money that would otherwise have been paid to the children, and to Uncle Sam in the form of taxes, will instead be paid to the bank amortizing the loan. The accompanying charts (See Charts 4.16, 4.17.) illustrate how borrowing funds to establish a Clifford Trust can accomplish satisfactory accumulation requirements for the parents. At the same time the plan improves cash flow while providing the required funds for educating children.

An attractive salary deferral program which is colloquially known as the 401K plan, a term from the Internal Revenue Code Section, presents another

Flow Of Funds For
Educational Expenses
(Using After Tax Income)

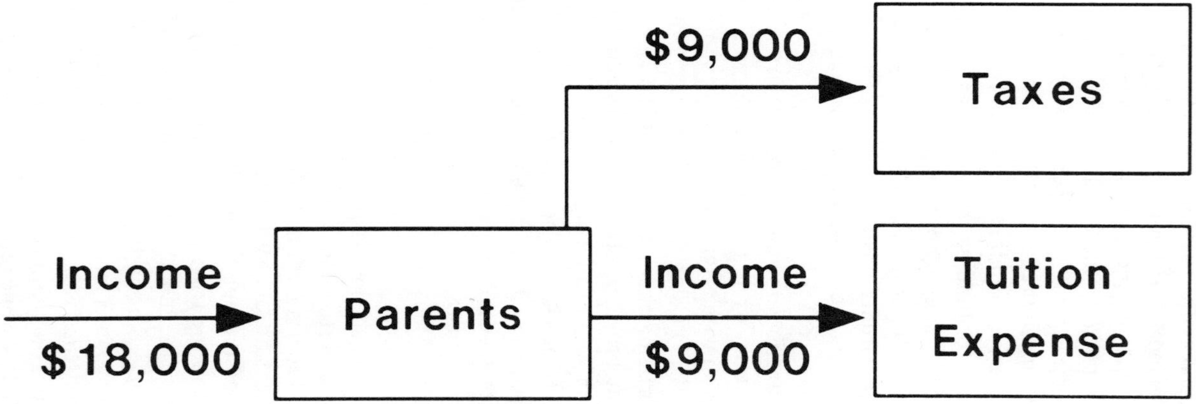

Income
$18,000

Parents

$9,000

Taxes

Income
$9,000

Tuition
Expense

● After Tax Disposable Income Used
To Meet Tuition Expense

CHART 4.13

John Doe
Cash Flow Statement

Total Direct Compensation		$120,000
Less:		
*Total Taxes		(39,939)
Disposable Income		$80,061
Less:		
Personal Living Expenses	$43,000	
Debt Payments	4,000	
Tuition Expense	9,000	
Savings Plan	4,000	
Lifestyle Depreciation Accrual	**	
Personal Liquidity Reserve	**	
Tax Reserve	**	(60,000)
Net Cash Flow		$20,061

*Net Itemized Deductions and Exemptions $18,000
** Cash Management System Considerations

CHART 4.14

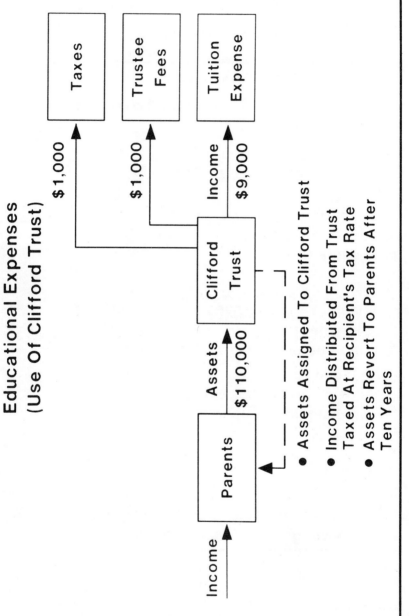

Flow Of Funds For
Educational Expenses
(Use Of Clifford Trust)

Income

Parents

Assets
$110,000

Clifford
Trust

Income
$9,000 → Tuition Expense

$1,000 → Trustee Fees

$1,000 → Taxes

- Assets Assigned To Clifford Trust
- Income Distributed From Trust Taxed At Recipient's Tax Rate
- Assets Revert To Parents After Ten Years

CHART 4.15

John Doe
Cash Flow Statement
With Clifford Trust

Total Direct Compensation		$120,000
Less:		
Total Taxes		(34,401)
Disposable Income		$ 85,599
Less:		
Personal Living Expenses	$43,000	
Debt Payments	16,740	
Tuition Expense	0	
Savings Plan	4,000	
Lifestyle Depreciation Accrual	–	
Personal Liquidity Reserve	–	
Tax Reserve	–	(63,740)
Net Cash Flow		$21,859
Clifford Trust Income		$11,000
Less:		
Total Taxes	$1,000	
Trustee Fees	1,000	(2,000)
Net Income		$ 9,000
Less:		
Tuition/Expense		(9,000)
Net Additional Income		$ 0

CHART 4.16

John Doe
Cash Flow Statement
With Salary Deferral Program
(401K)

Total Direct Compensation	$120,000
Less:	
Contributions to Savings	(8,000)
Reported Income	$112,000
Less:	
Total Taxes	(35,911)
Disposable Income	$76,089

Less:		
Personal Living Expenses	$43,000	
Debt Payments	4,000	
Tuition Expense	9,000	
Savings Plan	..	
Lifestyle Depreciation Accrual	...	
Personal Liquidity Reserve	...	
Tax Reserve	...	(56,000)
Net Cash Flow		$20,089

·Net Itemized Deductions and Exemptions $18,000
·· Saving Pre-Tax
··· Cash Management System Considerations

CHART 4.17

alternate use of cash-flow planning. The 401K's are available through many employers today. A self-employed person may also take advantage of similar benefits in a Keogh plan. An employee may contribute pre-tax dollars to this thrift savings plan and thereby substantially increase the amount that can be contributed or saved without impairing cash flow. Because of the tax-advantaged opportunity in the 401K, there's a certain financial magic which takes place when one accumulates pre-taxed dollars and compounds interest on those dollars *without* the income being taxed! (Charts 4.18 and 4.19)

Understanding and defining your cash flow while establishing a sound budget system each year in advance will not only improve your financial health and well being but also your family relationships. Too many family arguments and disagreements occur as a result of a lack of adequate cash-flow planning. Unrealistic and careless planning may often result in needless conflicts and misunderstandings within the family unit. People tend to underestimate the outflow and overestimate the timing or amount of the in-flow. This is a normal human failing, and the prudent planner must be aware of the pitfalls which are certain to occur when income and outgo estimates are carelessly calculated. Similarly, adequate provisions for liquidity or tax reserve requirements allowing for unexpected events and for depreciation of our material possessions will provide a sense of financial health and satisfaction. This positive result is something many people, unfortunately, have not yet experienced. It's one more intangible benefit from good financial planning. Most people do not feel good about themselves financially because they do not have enough money, which is another way of saying they do not have adequate liquidity provisions and lack sound cash-flow planning. It doesn't make much difference how many assets we have or how much income we receive; however, *it does matter* whether or not we have a well thought out plan providing for the unexpected and the unplanned event. Fear and apprehension generally result from lack of planning for taxes, unexpected depreciation, emergencies, changes in interest rates and/or investment timing and income. Following the steps and plans outlined in this chapter, I am hopeful, will help you overcome unexpected financial events in your life through careful anticipation and realistic planning. When you are prepared for the sudden jolts and the unexpected bumps of life you are able to cope with those financial displacements which tend to disturb those who are not as well prepared. The well-planned individual is usually rather serene—even while those around him are concerned, worried and even in a state of panic. Plan and keep cool.

TALE OF TWO EXECUTIVES

Several years ago I was counselling with several executives at a local company—a large Fortune 500 publicly traded corporation. Two executives stand out clearly in my memory—not because of their similarities so much as their differences.

John Doe
Cash Flow Statement
With Salary Deferral Program (401K)
And Clifford Trust

Total Direct Compensation		$120,000
Less:		
Contributions to Savings		(8,000)
Reported Income		$112,000
Less:		
˙Total Taxes		(35,911)
Disposable Income		$ 76,089
Less:		
Personal Living Expenses	$43,000	
Debt Payments	16,740	
Tuition Expense	0	
Savings Plan	˙˙	
Lifestyle Depreciation Accrual	˙˙˙	
Personal Liquidity Reserve	˙˙˙	
Tax Reserve	˙˙˙	(59,740)
Net Cash Flow		$21,784

˙Net Itemized Deductions and Exemptions $29,000
˙˙ Saving Pre-Tax
˙˙˙ Cash Management System Considerations

CHART 4.18

Net Cash Flow Comparisons
Alternatives For Funding Educational Expenses
And Funding Salary Deferral Program

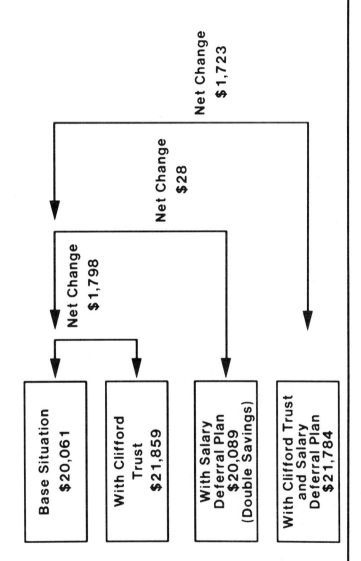

Base Situation
$20,061

With Clifford
Trust
$21,859

Net Change
$1,798

With Salary
Deferral Plan
$20,089
(Double Savings)

Net Change
$28

With Clifford Trust
and Salary
Deferral Plan
$21,784

Net Change
$1,723

CHART 4.19

At the time both executives had identical stock options. The men were earning similar salaries. Their ages were not more than two years apart. They had parallel educations, each holding an MBA from a top-rated university. However, that's where the similarities ended.

One executive, let's call him Smart, had, over the years, wisely provided for a $20,000 to $30,000 depreciation fund. His fund was mainly in CD's and T-Bills providing a strong positive cash flow. The other man, whom I'll refer to as Careless, had liquid assets of little more than $2,000 in his checking account. Careless had no other liquidity, no depreciation reserve and, on top of that, had incurred substantial bank debt funding some ill-advised tax shelters. Careless's credit was exhausted while Smart had no debt whatever.

Both agreed to exercise their options and each borrowed 100% of the required funds from a bank friendly to the corporation's executives. A large corporation's main banks go out of their way to curry favor with executives at the favored organization. Many times banks extend credit to these executives to the ultimate detriment of the individual. But, that's another point I address elsewhere. Back to our story:

Shortly after exercising the options the stock market took an adverse turn, something the market seems to always do at precisely the wrong time. The corporation's stock lost about 40% of its price with a month or two in the Bear market. That is, the market for the stock had fallen 40% *below* the price at which Smart and Careless had exercised their options. Naturally, the ever-so-friendly bank called upon the two executives to put up additional collateral supporting the stock loans. Smart was able to meet his margin call with assets in his depreciation fund. Careless had no alternative but to sell approximately 50% of his stock at the then depressed price. Remember, these two men had similar incomes, similar circumstances, identical stock, same lender and like margin calls. One was able to comfortably cope with the situation. The other was forced to take an undesirable and costly course of action.

A few years later the value of the stock more than recovered from the short-lived depressed period. In fact, the stock was now commanding *three* times the price Smart and Careless paid when exercising their options. Smart's holdings were worth three times what he paid for his shares. Careless had only half as many shares as Smart.

The difference boiled down to a simple matter of sound financial planning versus no planning; a case of discipline versus no discipline; an example of being prepared for whatever may occur and being exposed to the adverse winds of fate without a plan and without adequate liquidity.

At last report, Smart was still getting richer and richer while poor old Careless continued struggling to hold onto what he had. They are both going to reach retirement at about the same time. One is facing his golden years with confidence while the other has admitted to me, on more than one occasion, he's seriously concerned about the future. Even though Careless is now in his mid-fifties, I have a suggestion for him and other *Carelesses* of the world: It's never too late to stop being careless and start being smart.

Chapter Five

CREDIT: USE IT BUT DON'T ABUSE IT

The wise use of credit in a well structured personal financial strategy can become a valuable and important supplemental tool to aid in amortizing significant lifestyle requirements while permitting the planner to take advantage of timely investment opportunities. Throughout the financial life cycle you will find that credit plays a pivotal role. Think of credit in terms of two basic formats: consumer credit and investment credit.

Consumer Credit

Consumer credit is the type of credit allowing one to smooth out the up's and down's occurring with purchases of material goods and services of relatively large size or scope. As a rule major acquisitions do not comfortably permit full cash payment at the time of purchase. Obvious illustrations are the home, second home, major appliances and furniture, automobiles, boats, aircraft and other significant items. Most individuals start using consumer credit at the time of marriage, for wedding rings, as an example. The initial phases of our personal financial life cycle are usually heavily committed to the use of consumer credit. Over the past two decades, however, many lenders have extended traditional consumer credit to include month-to-month retail purchases through credit cards and department store charge accounts. This should be discouraged because of the relatively high costs associated with these forms of consumer credit. Instead, concentrate on the use of consumer credit through more sophisticated banking and/or retail credit lending sources. Be alert to the "true" cost of consumer financing.

I am thoroughly convinced that a much wiser and more comfortable financial lifestyle develops when one uses credit for the purchase of substantial consumer items rather than invading savings and liquidity. The liquidity levels discussed in previous chapters should be maintained because, generally speaking, we do not replace the liquidity when used for emergency or heavy consumer purchases. Using credit wisely by borrowing money and including the increased fixed expense (known as loan payments) in the cash distribution system, one will be able to maintain the desired liquidity level. We will thereby have protected our overall accumulation program while charging the expenditure to consumption rather than decreasing the level of savings.

The amount of consumer credit to utilize in this manner differs with each individual. Factors to consider include income, tax position, present cash-flow position, lifestyle requirements and personal needs.

For high tax bracket individuals or families, the use of consumer credit affords another distinct advantage. Normally, under current income tax laws, interest for consumer debt is deductible. Home mortgage interest and financing costs for automobiles, furniture and appliance loans are normally deductible in full from federal income tax. Moreover, the interest included for consumer debt is not considered in the calculation of the maximum investment interest which is deductible under current income tax law. The use of consumer debt, therefore, provides for greater tax deductions than may normally be allowable. Similarly, the amount or type of consumer debt will not normally influence your decision-making.

It is advantageous to develop a line of credit or master note for the potential and unforeseen needs. Your bank will provide a line of credit; you will sign a master note against which you may borrow and repay your loan from time to time. Normally there is no cost involved until you actually borrow funds.

With this ongoing line of bank credit the client is able to make expensive purchases at his discretion, repaying the loan as cash is available without having to execute new indebtedness papers with each transaction. Having a standby line of credit enables the borrower to negotiate the best possible "cash" price when making a major purchase.

Regardless of the mode of the creation of the obligation, it is usually a wise practice to avoid charge account and credit card credit. Establishing an ongoing line of credit, master note or individual borrowing arrangement with a qualified banking or credit institution is preferable and will involve less cost to the borrower. Interest costs will usually be less and your establishment of credit with institutions on which you may come to rely in the future will grow in value over the years. Some credit cards offer no-interest terms when paid within ten days, for example. In this case you have consumer credit at no cost.

Work backward from your cash management system to determine that you have adequate cash flow when considering the requirements funding discussed in the previous chapter. Review your plan before making additional credit obligations. If your cash flow can accommodate the additional fixed expense of consumer and repayment terms the use of consumer debt is generally wise and prudent. If, however, the increased debt obligation disturbs your cash management system and endangers your ability to provide adequate reserves or unduly constricts liquidity, additional planning must be considered.

You should, of course, avail yourself of each and every opportunity to use trade, retail and credit-card terms requiring *no interest*. Avoid, when possible, those calling for interest or other fees. For example, where there is no interest applicable on retail credit or credit cards for 30 days, take advantage of the interest-free period by properly timing purchases and payments. There are certain credit facilities and credit cards offered by various entities allowing for amortization of payments without interest. Be aware of these "free credit" devices. Other credit providers allow for a discount of 10% to 20% when paid within a certain time. Be alert to those. Some argue that utility bills do not actually allow discounts for prompt payment but rather provide a hidden penalty for late payment. Who cares? It's the net effect that counts.

Don't kid yourself. These *minor* savings add up. I have a client who has taken advantage of special "no service charge" offers made by newly opened banks seeking their initial depositor base. By maintaining those "free" accounts over the years the client estimates he has avoided at least $500 a year in normal services charges. That's $5,000 in 10 years.

Investment Debt

Investment debt is credit used to acquire investments. Note that I include the home in consumer debts simply because I personally do not consider the home to be a typical *investment*. You will recall from Chapter 1 my reference to a study undertaken to determine whether it was better for executives to own or lease their homes. The conclusion of the study revealed it would have been financially advantageous for a typical executive to have rented his home during the 30-year period from 1923 to 1953. Most people realize the subsequent 30-year period, from the early 50's to the early 80's, witnessed a substantial increase in home values. It would have been better for anyone to have owned a home during the past 30-year inflationary period. There is no question but that many homeowners have seen their property values double or triple in the past ten years. What the future holds in this area of home values is problematical. No doubt it will be different from the last thirty years. In some markets residential real estate values have decreased during the past year or two. The home remains a major consumption item. Not only the initial purchase but the cost of maintenance, insurance, debt service and taxes continue to make a heavy impression on a family's cash-flow requirements. Therefore, I consider the home to be a consumer item and part of the consumer debt program as opposed to viewing it as an investment. Investment debt, therefore, is that debt which is incurred for the purposes of typical investments.

Consider as a part of your investment debt any obligations such as participation in syndications or partnerships, even though you may be only a limited partner in either. The amount of investment debt and the interest deducted therefrom are limited under current and proposed income tax legislation. The amount of interest you may deduct for income tax purposes on investment debt is limited to the amount of investment income you have. Excessive interest will be nondeductible; therefore it is lost as an income tax deduction.

The amount of investment that can be handled by anyone is determined by several factors: income, net cash flow, tax position, credit availability, income from passive investments as well as willingness of creditors to supply the credit. The amount of investment credit must be determined by working backwards from your cash management system. Look first at your net cash flow to determine the amount of cash available to service the anticipated investment credit. Then look at your distribution system to determine which portions of your overall cash management system will be affected by the anticipated debt service. Interest-only loans or balloon notes, i.e., loans where payments are small in early years and either balloon in the final year to very large amounts or escalate over the years, can be extremely hazardous. No investment loan should be undertaken based solely on repayment coming from the sale of the asset for which the investment loan is being incurred. One must have a clearly defined plan for repaying an investment loan. Repayment should come from other cash sources which may include income from the contemplated investment, but not from the *sale* of the investment alone.

Examples of the possible dire consequences resulting from ignoring this basic rule abound. Consider the difficulties which developed as a result of the 1980's so-called oil glut. The fall-out in oil prices not only adversely affected refiners and distributors but put serious crimps in the drilling industry. As the entire energy universe suffered, so did commercial real estate—especially in areas where energy companies were located. Drilling companies owed secured notes equalling two and three times the market values of rigs. It's no wonder so many were thrown into Chapter 11 Bankruptcy. Banks across the country still have rigs in storage, slowly rusting away. Vacant office buildings stand as monuments to booms gone bust. How could these problems have been averted, you ask?

Instead of worrying about how some drilling company or real estate promoter may have avoided bankruptcy, let's use these illustrations as guideposts for your own personal financial planning. Consider:

● When borrowing or financing an acquisition, have a clearly defined repayment plan—including contingency plans. Remember Smart who exercised those stock options with 100% bank financing? He had liquid reserves to protect his position. Careless did not. Smart had alternatives.

- Be especially cautious when investing in raw and unimproved land. There's no cash flow as a rule, and certainly not enough for full debt service.
- Assume the loan will have to be repaid, at least in part, by assets *other* than that which collateralizes the loan. If the collateral actually retires the debt, be thankful you did not have to call on other assets. The Boy Scouts have a slogan we can all benefit from: Be Prepared.

Every successful leveraged buy-out I have studied involved one or more optional plans of action. As a rule, the investor was sooner or later called on to take an alternative course due to circumstances which were allowed for at the time of the buy-out but not expected to occur. An individual buying a property or entering into an investment should not approach the acquisition any differently from the way professionals design and finance leveraged buy-outs. Individuals can learn much about credit from a study of the way successful corporate financiers structure their loans and repayments.

It is also important for an investor to pre-determine a reasonable period of time during which an investment loan will be retired. That is, you should not anticipate your bank or credit institution being able or willing to accommodate a continuation or extension of an investment loan. Also, moving a loan from one lending institution to another is risky and costly, and an example of poor credit planning. This evidences weak financial discipline as well as unsatisfactory credit usage. Refinancing has caused severe credit displacement within the financial structure of individuals and has been a major factor in causing good plans to turn sour. The family cash flow and financial asset accumulative powers may also be frustrated through the repeated renewal of a loan. The wise use of investment credit can, of course, leverage your income and/or your assets and provide for a multiple expansion of your overall net worth. Likewise, improper or unplanned use of investment debt can cause severe shrinkage in net worth. If cash flow and/or other lifestyle requirements have not allowed for investment debt, the assumption of new debt can result in the necessity of redesigning the overall plan.

Remember, plan to pay investment debt from *other* assets or from future income before incurring the obligation. Be certain you are willing to lose money as well as make a profit before incurring investment debt. All investments involve an element of risk, and the chances of loss in many are greater than the odds of gain. Awareness of the risk factor is particularly important as you move through the survival period and into the accumulation or preservation periods of your personal financial life cycle. When there is the opportunity to lose, and all investments contain such possibilities, you are dealing with a double-edged sword. Be cautious when assuming additional debt for investment purposes. One must also recognize that an investment always sounds best when entering into it. Investments do not always prove to be satisfactory from an anticipated overall economic standpoint, or more particularly, the timing of the investment does not always prove to be in keeping with original projections. Seldom does any investment come up to the expectations of the investor. Therefore, additional funds may have to be committed in order to maintain the investment, avoid sacrificing value or suffering immediate loss. Some investments require time to work out—usually a great deal more time than first anticipated. You should, therefore, be prepared not only to incur obligations and/or debt to make the initial investment. Anticipate delay, additional costs, higher interest rates and other negatives. Remember Murphy's Law: If anything can go wrong, it probably will. Be prepared to incur additional debt and costs or be willing and able to utilize other resources in the process, including your time. Failure to identify and understand this risk/reward potential is often the cause of financial failure of a given investment.

There are two key overall considerations in credit usage which are important for each family's consideration.

First, consumer or investment debt should not be incurred without adequate liquidity, cash flow and credit availability relationships. To put it another way, a frequent cause of bankruptcy and/or investment or business failure occurs when the obligator has used all of the credit resources available from any one source. Retail, consumer and/or commercial debts have little or no liquidity value and result in a poor or negative cash flow. In such circumstances the individual is not able to cope with an upturn in interest rates or a decrease in the value of the collateral underlying the debt. When the investor is faced with forced debt reduction without liquidity or adequate cash flow to meet the obligation he may be forced to sell assets in an adverse market—resulting in substantial losses. When overly extended the individual usually cannot survive the repayment pressures and will ultimately be forced to loss or even bankruptcy. It is imperative, therefore, before undertaking substantial amounts of investment debt and/or consumer debt that one preserve and protect liquidity as discussed in the previous chapter. Understand cash flow and be cautious not to overestimate the anticipated cash value or fail to adequately allow ample timing of results from investments. To the contrary, one should *overestimate* the length of time it may take for an investment to bear fruit and *underestimate* the ultimate outcome of the investment. In any event, be certain credit is kept in context. Don't be impulsive with credit. Be sure you can afford it rather than using credit to make possible something you otherwise could not afford.

Second, consider your tolerance for debt. Earlier we discussed an examination of attitudes towards debt and risk as you develop your personal financial strategy. The use of credit is perhaps the most important factor one may utilize in determining the relative value of incremental asset accumulation through the leveraging of income and assets. The relative risk of losing what you have through the incurrence of new debt may cause loss of other assets. Your lifestyle may be depressed; you may miss future investment opportunities by *amortizing* debt losses for investments that did not pay off as anticipated. If you find upon careful and objective examination that you cannot tolerate debt or that you cannot comfortably assume risks involved, then stay away from debt as a means of accumulating assets. Often this is a serious focal point of husband/wife conflicts. It makes no difference how good the investment may be or the ability of the family to handle debt from the financial point of view if, emotionally and psychologically, another member of the family cannot comfortably accept the use of debt in overall financial management. Agreement by the husband and wife in this area can prevent many an emotional and family problem as well as avoid financial catastrophe due to lack of cooperation within the marital team for specific financial objectives.

One last caveat: Credit can be an important family financial disciplinary tool when used wisely. Credit may enable one to accumulate both better quality consumer items as well as acquire important and profitable investments. Normally, you will meet loan obligations whereas you may not continue to voluntarily save or accumulate in an orderly fashion. When used as a financial disciplinary tool the family may benefit through the wise use of credit. Tolerance and discipline and understanding can produce dramatic results from leveraging both income and assets but only after you consider the various factors mentioned.

One last thought. Additional amounts of life, disability and liability insurance should be considered during periods of heavy investment or consumer credit. Through the use of insurance one may substitute protection for debt repayment, retirement and cash receipts that would be unobtainable otherwise. The family may suffer severe financial and economic displacement by having to sell assets in adverse markets due to an untimely physical disability or unforeseen litigation judgments. There are many forms of insurance protection available. In some cases you may view certain insurance plans as a means of protection from loss due to consumer and investment credit.

I am deeply concerned about the possible adverse consequences occurring when executives use extensive amounts of credit while in the employ of a major company. Banks have a tendency to indulge executives in whatever credit amounts the executive desires. This results in two serious potential problems: (1) The amount of credit may not be justified, and (2) in the event the employee separates from the employer, the bank will likely view the credit differently—thus putting undue pressure on the borrower. Consider the following actual case:

One of my clients, a senior vice president of a major company, exercised a rather substantial stock option by borrowing the needed funds from a local bank—a bank which, by the way, was the principal lending institution for the company where the executive was employed. The loan involved the typical understanding and arrangements usually made with executives of a corporation doing business with the lender. As a rule, the interest rate in these "friendly" situations is an attractive fraction-over-prime. The stock purchased under the option constituted the sole collateral for the loan. Since the stock could not be considered as *total* collateral under SEC rules, a portion of the loan was, in fact, unsecured.

Shortly after the exercise of the option, the executive left that company for other employment. The new employer was not a customer of the bank which had made the loan. The lending bank then, of course, took a different position and a less favorable attitude with respect to the executive's loan. At the first renewal date the interest rate was substantially increased and an accelerated repayment schedule demanded. The bank's action resulted in the executive being forced to increase his cash-flow obligations to meet the new amortization schedule and the higher interest payments. Fortunately, the executive had made adequate liquidity provisions and was able to accommodate the bank's demands. Thus he avoided the necessity of selling the stock prematurely. His comment to me, however, was, "I never realized how banks' friendliness can change, depending on your connections."

When dealing with banks—especially in connection with lines of credit and loans—remember bank policy as well as bankers' attitudes tend to change. When negotiating bank loans, it is advisable to *assume* the friendly banker's attitude will, sooner or later, change. If you sell your company, change jobs, move your CD's or reduce the average balance carried in your non-interest checking account, you can be darn sure things *will* change—and not in your favor. Bank on it.

You can protect yourself from changing banking tides and attitudes by negotiating the longest possible terms when borrowing funds. As a general rule, a loan's terms cannot be altered or amended until the note comes due or at time for renewal. For example, it is far better from your point of view to sign a three-year installment note than to sign a 90-day note with understandings that the loan *may* be renewed a dozen times giving you three years to repay. *Something* could occur in the meantime. The bank has the right to demand full payment at the next due date. So long as payments are made on time on your 36-month note, you have the right to take the full term to pay. Of course, it's wise to have a prepayment provision enabling you to pay the note early if you so elect. But it's your option—not the bank's.

Chapter Six

INSURANCE: PROTECTION AGAINST THE UNFORESEEN

Insurance has never been more important than it is today. There are dozens of ways modern insurance plans may be used in protecting what you have. This includes your life, your property, your income, your health and even your estate after you are gone from this earth. Insurance embodies two important basics: (1) an insurable risk, and (2) making certain that which is financially uncertain. *Guaranty* is synonymous with insurance.

Before proceeding further into the subject of insurance, I'll share with you a basic definition of the term:

> INSURANCE—An arrangement, usually in the form of a contract, whereby an insuror (insurance company) agrees to protect an insured person or business against a *catastrophic* loss in exchange for payment of premium or premiums.

I emphasize *catastrophic* because if there is not an element of *substantial* loss or risk, insurance is not a necessity and it need not be considered in a financial plan. For example, *you* should carry the small or minor risks, that is, the risks you can afford. A young person with limited resources should consider buying collision insurance on his or her personal automobile. For this person, the loss of the vehicle would be a truly catastrophic loss. However, I have many clients who are older and who are in the financial position of being self-insurors of their automobiles. I am thinking of one individual in particular. He says he has been self-insuring the collision coverage on his cars for more than ten years. When calculating the amount of premiums he would have been paying for protection, he says he could afford to suffer a total loss every three years and still come out dollars ahead. As a matter of fact, during the ten years he has been self-insuring his automobiles, he has had two minor losses: a hit-and-run incident which cost $1,700 to repair and a fender-bender which set him back $550. By self-insuring this client has saved approximately $3,500 in yearly premiums.

As we proceed through this chapter on insurance keep the definition in mind as well as the points illustrated in this example.

Insurable Risk

In order to buy any form of insurance the purchaser must be able to show that the beneficiary has an insurable interest in what is being insured. It must be shown that a material loss would be incurred if something harmful happened to the object of the coverage. The principle of insurance, simply stated, is that it enables us to protect ourselves against the unforeseen and unexpected. Insurance may be used to smooth out the extremes of our financial existence by providing coverage in the event of loss—and loss may come in many forms: death, disability, storm, fire, burglary, flood—you name it. These are the risks we may elect to protect ourselves from through insurance.

Certainty out of Uncertainty

Making certain that which is uncertain is an important adjunct to our entire financial life cycle. The young couple requires adequate insurance to protect them against early death of the breadwinner (or breadwinners), loss of property due to theft or fire, loss of income, hospitalization and a multitude of other hazards. While in the accumulation or preservation stages needs for insurance continue for the same basic reasons. Also, in later stages it is obvious protection is needed for the unforeseen, unexpected or estate taxes, especially if the breadwinner meets an early and untimely death. Liability claims and liquidity needs due to heavy debt assumptions are other risks which may be provided for through insurance plans.

There are four basic types of insurance which concern the family or individual financial planner: life insurance, disability and health insurance, liability protection, property and casualty insurance.

LIFE INSURANCE

As the name implies, this form of insurance covers the life of an individual and may be purchased in three broad policy formats, or in combinations of the three formats. (Chart 6.1) We take a closer look at whole life and term life here. Endowments and annuities, the third class of life insurance, are mentioned later.

Whole Life Insurance

Premiums are divided among the cost of the risk and additions to cash value. Whole life insurance provides a forced savings plan which is what builds the cash values, while whole life should be thought of as a form of insurance providing partial investment or savings opportunities through the accumulation of cash values. Many times, however, it is advantageous to purchase whole life insurance and pay for it through what is commonly known as a minimum deposit program. In this method of providing life insurance protection the owner of the insurance actually borrows the cash value to reduce costs or to pay premiums. Under current law the interest on the policy loan is deductible for income tax purposes. The net effect of owning a whole life policy while using or borrowing the cash value to pay premiums reduces the net cost of the policy, and in some instances the cost may actually be less than term insurance prices. A trained and qualified life insurance agent can fully explain the mechanics of the minimum deposit plans.

Term Life Insurance

This form of life insurance contract provides for "pure" protection. The premiums paid are applied *only* to the cost of risk, and generally the cost increases with age. There is no cash value accumulation, no forced savings element. Term insurance is pure and simple "death" insurance. Term insurance may be convertible to whole life or some other forms of insurance usually without proof of insurability at some point during the life of the contract. Term insurance is generally the lowest cost life insurance policy available.

While term insurance may be lower in cost than the whole life minimum deposit combination in early years, the whole life minimum deposit program may prove to be less costly as the age of the insured advances. This is due to the higher cost of premiums for term insurance at advanced ages.

There are many variations to these two basic forms of life insurance. Some term insurance, for example, may decrease in face value over a period of years—called decreasing term insurance. Some term policies provide for annual renewability to age 65 without proof of insurability.

Other contracts provide for paid-up life insurance contracts. The premium must be paid for a certain number of years after which the policy is fully paid and the face value of the policy will be paid at the insured's death. The cash value on this type of contract may be withdrawn from the policy by the owner of the contract as values increase. Paid-up life insurance is a ready-made line of credit for the policyowner. Low-interest policy loans may be made with no questions asked, no collateral.

77

Life Insurance

Whole-Life

- Premiums Partly For Cost Of Risk And Partly Add To Cash Value
- Forced Savings Plan
- An Investment

Term

- Premiums Only Cost Of Risk And Increase With Age
- No Cash Value
- Pure Insurance

Variations

- Group Term, Decreasing Term, Level Term, Annual Renewability, Convertibility, Minimum Deposit, Whole Life, Paid Up, Waiver Of Premiums

CHART 6.1

Considerations for Determining the Amount of Life Insurance

Your life insurance program should be considered in the aggregate. The amount of insurance provided by your employer benefit programs together with your veteran's life insurance or U.S. Government life insurance programs should be considered as you develop a personal life insurance program. Your employer life insurance plan should be carefully examined to determine the amount, if any, of protection carried forward *after* retirement. Many group term programs provided by employers either terminate at retirement or substantially reduce within a few years after retirement. Some plans rapidly decline to a very nominal amount or none at all. You may also have a one-time opportunity to convert your group life insurance to a personal contract, but the rates at the advanced retirement age are normally prohibitive for economic conversion to be undertaken, that is, unless you are uninsurable, in which case life insurance at any price may be a bargain.

If your employer group life insurance terminates with your retirement or declines substantially thereafter, you should maintain a personal insurance program of sufficient magnitude to cover debts and some, if not all, of your potential estate tax liabilities which come due at your death. Other important considerations are (1) the amount of debt you are presently carrying for investment and consumer debt; (2) the number of dependents in your family, both present and potential due to health, age and education situations; (3) the amount of estate tax due at death. Also, when designing a life insurance program the liquid and non-liquid nature of your estate should be estimated. If most of your estate is in real estate or other assets which are relatively nonliquid, such as a closely held business which will likely take a great deal of time to sell, the greater the amount of life insurance you should carry. If most of your estate is in liquid assets such as marketable stocks, bonds and CD's, then your life insurance requirements are somewhat less. It is not unusual for persons over age 65 with a sound financial plan in effect to have little or no need for life insurance protection.

For a young couple the income requirements of the surviving spouse are extremely important and are needs easily met by life insurance. If the surviving spouse is economically self-sufficient through income-earning power the needed amount of life insurance is less. Obviously, if there are minors involved Social Security provides for income payments until the youngest reaches 18 years of age. The amount of life insurance should be increased depending upon the number of children and the expenses projected in connection with their education and lifestyle requirements.

The ownership of life insurance is as important as the amount and type of policies selected. There are several important considerations which are generally overlooked or, in many instances, are not given proper consideration. Life insurance is an asset just like any other part of your overall estate. The insured person is normally the owner although ownership may be transferred to another. You should check your existing policies to determine the legal owner of the policy. For instance, insurance will be taxed in the estate of the owner, not necessarily the estate of the insured. If you want to avoid estate taxation on your life insurance in your estate, a trust or another person should own the insurance policies on your life.

By the same token, your beneficiary designation should be considered carefully and should be coordinated with the overall estate plan including provisions under your will. Too often the wrong beneficiary is designated under the insured's policies with counter-productive results such as unintentionally naming an ex-wife or a business associate with whom no present business relationships are involved. These unfortunate situations generally occur due to oversight and the failure to regularly and systematically review the life insurance portfolio.

Be certain your beneficiary will receive funds as part of your overall estate planning program, not on top of or instead of your otherwise-intended beneficiary designations. Similarly, you should see that beneficiary designations provide the necessary liquidity to the executor of your will for the intended purposes of paying debts and taxes. That is, if such is the purpose of owning the insurance policy in the first place.

You should also consider the amount of life insurance in the context of income replacement potential. That is, the face amount of insurance times the estimated return on the insurance proceeds when taken as income less taxes, if any, to be paid provide a pre-determined income to your beneficiaries replacing all or a portion of income lost through death.

On the other hand, the amount of your insurance can be an important estate protection device. If you are careful to calculate the estimated transfer taxes to be applied to your estate, you can provide funds for *all* tax obligations through a well-planned life insurance program.

And you should always be aware of the taxability of the proceeds of the insurance. Determine the net amount of life insurance proceeds available to your executors and/or your beneficiaries for the intended purpose of either income replacement through investment or estate and asset protection by covering transfer taxes. Properly structured, life insurance proceeds can totally escape taxation. At the same time life insurance coverage can enable you to leave a tax-free estate.

You should regularly monitor your life insurance policies and the premium costs. Today there are many new forms of life insurance: variable premium, variable cost, universal life plans, variable cash accumulations and variable investment programs under the cash value provisions. There is no single life insurance policy suitable for all persons or all situations. Similarly, insurance purchased over past years may be higher cost insurance than what is available today through competitive modern policies. Often you are able to substantially increase your life insurance protection without paying more dollars than you've been paying for years. Inversely, you may be able to substantially reduce the amount of costs and maintain the same amount of life insurance coverage. In any event, like other elements of personal finance, life insurance needs (i.e., contracts selected, premiums paid, ownership and beneficiary designations) and purposes change as the economy and your family changes. When your asset and debt structures alter your life insurance requirements also change. Be on top of your insurance plans and monitor the total portfolio carefully year by year.

Can you imagine the heartbreak, bitterness and confusion which occurs when a man dies and his life insurance policies are payable to an ex-wife; and the present wife is left with nothing? This situation occurs more often than we would like to admit. Believe it or not—it happens every day.

Under old laws there were certain advantages from a tax point of view for cross-ownership of life insurance policies. For example, the husband was the owner of life insurance covering his wife's life. She was the owner of the policy insuring his life. In these cases the owner would also be the beneficiary. As tax laws changed, the advantages of cross-ownership became less important. Yet today many husbands still own the wife's policy and vice versa. The problems become acute when following a divorce, couples never get around to changing life insurance policies. Thus the strange and tragic case of Mr. Thoughtless who dies and leaves a substantial insurance estate to the *first* Mrs. T. while the present wife goes empty-handed. As a financial counsellor I witness this cruel occurrence far too often. It's a typical example of carelessness in planning (or I should say, the lack of planning) leading to unnecessary loss of funds at the very time a widow desperately needs resources. An astute and cautious counsellor would never allow this to occur.

The astute and thoughtful individual will completely and thoroughly review life insurance on an annual basis. Ownership and beneficiary designations must be reviewed periodically. Also, many life insurance policies contain options and rights which are time-sensitive. For example, at certain intervals the owner of a particular life insurance policy may be able to increase coverage without evidence of insurability. Annual reviews prevent the possible loss of valuable rights and options due to oversight.

Establish a yearly date for reviewing your life insurance policies. It may be January 1, your birthday, July 4 or whatever date you find easy to remember. Be certain you never overlook your annual policy review date. If everyone would follow this simple rule the case of an ex-wife or former business associate collecting life insurance proceeds intended for a present wife would become a rare occurrence.

DISABILITY AND HEALTH

Through disability insurance one can provide *income* protection in the event of disability. (Chart 6.2) For example, when one is unable to perform his or her duties as a professional, employee, or manager of a business, disability income coverage can be a godsend. Too often we find this important form of

Disability Income Protection

- Provide A Current Income To Replace Vocational Income

- Considerations:

  Current Lifestyle Costs, Debt Service, Future Obligation Accruals (College), Inflation

CHART 6.2

insurance has been overlooked by our clients when we review a new client's overall insurance program. The potential for an individual under sixty becoming severely disabled is far greater than the risk of premature death. The amount of insurance provided for disability should be consistent with probability and risk.

The amount of disability income protection should take into account the following considerations. First, what are your current lifestyle costs, i.e., how much is the overhead? How much would it cost you to live as you are now living? Do you desire to maintain this lifestyle should you become totally and permanently disabled? How much would your overhead decrease if you were not active in your profession, business or vocation? How much, on the other hand, would costs increase without your services and skills? Do you want your family to maintain a lifestyle similar to that which it presently enjoys? Disability income provides answers to these troubling questions.

Second, what is the amount of debt you are carrying and what debt service costs do you have on an annual and/or monthly basis that would continue even though your income stopped due to disability? The higher the debt service, obviously the higher the amounts of disability income protection needed.

Third, what are your future obligation accruals, such as college education for your children, care for elderly parents or handicapped members of the family? The higher these accruals are, or the potential accruals, the more coverage you should consider acquiring in your disability insurance program.

Fourth, the purchasing power of a dollar should be carefully considered when ongoing inflation is a factor. The amount of your disability income protection should be increased as you move along the financial life cycle. Most disability income plans allow for the puchase of riders which are options for added policy limits. They are known as Guaranteed Insurability Riders.

Fifth, you should also consider the amount of your passive income from accumulated investments and disability income provided by your employer benefit plans. Most thrift savings as well as pension benefits vest automatically in the event of total and permanent disability. Social Security benefit payments are payable in the event of total disability. You may also be eligible for provisions for disability under the terms of private benefit programs and workers' compensation.

I cannot emphasize enough the need for your careful attention and thorough consideration of disability income protection. More often than not, we find people are better prepared to die than to live with a disability. The latter, however, can be more disastrous to a family than death since ongoing expenses increase rather than decrease when total and permanent disability occurs. There's more need for income at a time when there is no income at all.

LIABILITY INSURANCE

As you move through the personal financial life cycle, the amounts of liability insurance you should carry will vary with real or potential liability exposure. Liability coverage protects both you and your family. (Chart 6.3) Most homeowner's policies under your property insurance contracts and automobile insurance contracts provide for certain minimums of liability coverage. In the event a third party is injured while visiting your home he may file a claim. Liability insurance protects you. While operating your automobile you are at risk, especially in the event of an accident. Liability coverage, while usually adequate in the early stages of the financial life cycle, may become totally inadequate as your assets and/or net worth increases. Therefore, it is extremely important that you consider the purchase of what is known as an umbrella liability policy or extended coverage liability coverage which in most states carries a nominal cost. This form of overall—thus the name, umbrella—protection picks up where your homeowner and automobile liability limits terminate. Generally speaking, you should keep your liability protection well out in front of your net worth; e.g., if your net worth is $500,000 you would want to have coverage of up to a million dollars. At all times you should have liability protection *greater* than your total net worth.

Be certain your business property liability coverage is adequate and/or provided for in separate contracts, that is, other than your personal homeowner, automobile or umbrella liability policies. As a rule, liability for business activity and/or actions involving a business operation are not covered under your personal homeowner, automobile and umbrella policies. The amount of liability insurance in connection with your business properties will be determined by the various risks involved and your responsibilities thereunder. Obviously your risks are substantially greater if you are operating as a proprietor or a partner than would be the case under certain types of incorporated business activities. In any event, as you move along the financial life cycle and your assets grow and/or business activity increases, pay increasing attention to your needs for adequate liability coverage. This is an important step in protecting what you have and may make the difference between a progressive estate accumulation program and one encumbered by severe setbacks due to unforeseen liability claims and/or litigation judgments. Another way to view liability coverage is the fact that the insurance company is obligated to defend you in the event of a claim. It's like having "legal" or "lawyer" insurance at no added cost.

PROPERTY AND CASUALTY INSURANCE

Property and casualty insurance involves protecting you and your property against catastrophic loss of assets due to such hazards as fire, storm, accident and burglary. (Chart 6.4)

Liability Insurance

- **Homeowner Liability**

- **Automobile Liability**

- **Umbrella Liability**

- **Business Properties Liability**

CHART 6.3

Property Insurance

- Protection Against Catastrophic Loss Of Assets

- Percentage Of Value Insured (Co-Insurance)

- Replacement Cost Riders

- Inventories (Pictorial)

- Scheduled Properties

- Rates

CHART 6.4

You should be certain you maintain the required percentage of value insured, i.e., that the minimum of insurance coverage on your home, automobile or other property as a stated percentage of the market value of the asset involved. If you fail to buy adequate coverage you may be co-insuring part of any claim with your insurance carrier. In other words, you will not be fully covered, and you may be insuring a larger portion than necessary. Next, you should carefully review your policies to determine whether you have *replacement cost riders*. Under modern insurance contracts in most states replacement cost coverage is available at affordable costs. Without replacement cost coverage you will be afforded only the depreciated value of any asset loss due to fire, burglary or accident. Your drapes which have been hanging for ten years, for example, will be valued at a very nominal amount for insurance coverage should fire destroy them. If, however, you have replacement cost coverage, then the drapes will be replaced at their current replacement cost. Adding the replacement cost riders provides a substantial difference in coverage and is available in most states for rather nominal increases in insurance premiums.

I strongly recommend you maintain a current inventory of all of the furniture and fixtures in your home, office and second home. It is generally a good idea not only to list the items and their values but to make photographs of each room. You should also have current photographs of such items as crystal, china, silverware, art and jewelry. In the event of loss, a picture will define worth better than a physical description alone. You should maintain the pictures and the inventory of properties some place other than the location of the property. I had a client a few years ago who did all the right things in preparing the inventory and making photos of all valuables and then left the prints in his bureau drawer. The home burned down and so did the inventory and pictures. We won the battle but lost the war in that instance.

You should be certain to schedule those properties which have the greatest probability of being stolen or lost. Often extensive scheduling of everything of sufficient value becomes prohibitive under your homeowner's insurance policies or even your business policies. Those items which are the most frequently lost or are most easily stolen such as cameras, items of jewelry, small antique items and objects of art should be scheduled.

You should monitor the rates you are paying under your insurance contracts. Rates vary in many instances from state to state but often you can provide varying amounts of insurance coverage depending upon how you handle the schedules in your policies as well as the riders you have. The deductible under such provisions as collision in your automobile insurance will vary depending upon your ability to assume part of the risk and a portion of the loss. For example, there is no sound reason to maintain a very low amount of deductible if your income, cash flow and asset accumulation permit you to sustain a heavier than minimum collision loss. The rates substantially decrease as the deductible increases. Insurance premiums should be considered as part of your fixed costs under your cash management program and should afford you additional peace of mind once adequate coverage has been provided on your life, property, income and for general liability protection. You will thus be able to assume debt, enhance your lifestyle and sustain your investments knowing you are protected against the unforeseen through a carefully planned insurance program.

REVIEW

Care should be taken when choosing a beneficiary of life insurance. Too often the executor finds himself in the awkward position of having to borrow money from the widow. It is generally traumatic for the wife to receive the life insurance and then be forced to loan it back to the estate. Alternate plans should be made for the use or disposition of life insurance when the cash proceeds are destined to accomplish purposes other than investments for the benefit of the surviving spouse.

I recall two individuals who suffered the loss of their homes by fire. In both cases the homes contained many valuable pieces of furniture, jewelry, furs, silver, art and antiques. In one case the homeowner had taken the precaution of videotaping the entire home and its contents. The 45-minute tape covered every inch of the property including all crystal, china, silver and other valuables. He had placed one copy of the tape in his bank safety deposit box and kept a second copy in his office.

The other individual made photographs of his property but had carelessly placed the photos along with the negatives in his bedroom dresser drawer. Of course, when the house went up in flames so did the photographs.

The first man was able to quickly and satisfactorily settle his claim thanks to the videotape. Also, because this homeowner had added a *replacement cost rider* to his policy, he was able to settle based on the current replacement cost—not the depreciated value of the lost property.

The second man—the one who no longer had pictorial records—did not have replacement coverage and was able to collect benefits based on the *estimated depreciated* value of the destroyed items. It took him much longer to establish his losses and settle his claim than the first man. The ultimate amount collected by the two were many, many thousands of dollars apart even though the values of the two properties and their contents were quite similar.

POINTS TO REMEMBER: Make an inventory and support it with photos. Snapshots are fine; videotapes are best. Have up-to-date appraisals of valuables such as paintings, furs, silver and jewelry and keep the appraisals, along with the inventory and photos, in a location other than that of the insured property. Update the photos and inventory at least once every three years and when major items are acquired.

Insurance is an important part of the total financial plan. However, it is probably an element which is more often mishandled, misunderstood and mistreated. Some individuals are "insurance poor"—they have the wrong policies, pay too much and fail to properly review coverage on a timely basis. Others are grossly *underinsured* which is another way of saying they are overexposed to potential catastrophic losses. Unless you have recently reviewed your total coverage, odds are you are in one of the previously-mentioned groups. That's the last place you want to be.

Chapter 7

INVESTMENTS: RATING THEM BY RISK VERSUS REWARD

A thorough study of the financial planning processes would not be complete without devoting a substantial portion of our attention to the study of investments. However, the word *investment* is a much too broadly used word in my judgment. And, to compound the situation, we must differentiate between *investment* and the active verb form *to invest*. Nevertheless, they have a common denominator. Both *investments* and *to invest* involve risk. In an economic sense, whenever risk is present there's also the possibility of a *reward,* thus the well-established risk/reward ratio.

Before we explore the various forms of investments and their attendant risks and before you undertake an investment program, you must satisfy five important prerequisites.

- Have a clear, fully understood perspective of the overall personal financial plan
- Be disciplined in the maintenance of adequate liquidity levels while implementing the financial plan
- Define and plan cash flow
- Use credit wisely—not excessively
- Provide the necessary insurances

Occupational Risk Vs. Investment Risk

Occupational Risk:
The Necessary Risks Taken To Create Capital

Investment Risk:
The Risk Taken During The Employment Of Capital To Create A Return On Such Investment

CHART 7.1

92

When you have taken these steps in your planning process, you are ready to move into the investment area.

Before exploring various forms of investment risks, first consider the relationship of occupational (or vocational) risk versus investment risk. (See Chart 7.1.) When considering occupational risk we look at the matter of how we are *to invest,* i.e., how shall we invest resources such as time, study and planning in our careers or professions. The occupational risk equates to action taken to *create* capital. It is the vocational hazard which we encounter when maintaining employer, client or customer relationships. The occupational risk is clearly evident if you are in business for yourself. For those persons actively practicing a profession it would be fair to consider the occupational risk as being the *professional* risk. These are risks and hazards knowingly and willingly undertaken to gain and maintain income and/or capital. Naturally it is your intention to make your capital grow into more formative amounts as you perfect the investment tactics of *your* financial plan. We shall cover these tactics and the risks *they* involve. Before we do, let's be sure we clearly understand the occupational risks and how they relate to investment risks.

Some think of occupational risks as being the same as *accumulation* risks. Either term is acceptable and both adequately define the sort of risks referred to. Occupational or accumulation risks involve the assumption that you will earn money from your labors. For some the money comes in the form of salary, commission or bonus paid by an employer. For the self-employed, it's the profit earned from the enterprise; and for the professional, it's the net proceeds of the practice or the amount of funds distributed among partners. There are certain accumulation or occupational hazards which must be recognized. These risks may be reduced or minimized to the extent the individual has skills and knowledge in his or her chosen field. For example, consider two newly licensed medical doctors: One may elect to become a specialist while the other may prefer to practice general medicine. Each has clearly made a choice regarding the occupational or professional risk. If the one who elected to be a specialist finds he has chosen a field which has also been selected by an excessive number of other physicians, his rewards may prove to be disappointingly smaller than anticipated. The general practitioner may discover there is a severe shortage of GP's. Therefore, the well qualified and successful general practitioner may be able to command a much larger income than the specialist. Of course, it's equally possible the specialist will earn more than the GP. You can, I am sure, think of dozens of other parallels which prove the point that there are risks involved when we choose a line of work, when we select the type or size of company we go to work for, or when making any career choices. The same risk-reward elements apply to the self-employed and the entrepreneur. All of the many critical occupational choices we make regarding how we will *invest* our time and energy will have a direct bearing on how much money we will earn. And our levels of earnings have a great deal to do with how many assets we have for investments.

It is not unusual nowadays for employees to quit their jobs and go into business for themselves. They usually do this with the expectation of earning more money. Some professionals leave their callings to go into business or become employees. In these examples each is making an *occupational risk choice.*

While many people assume that investment hazards entail greater risks than those associated with the occupational or accumulation phases, I am convinced the opposite is true.

My challenge, as a financial counsellor advising my clients, is to make clear the utmost importance of understanding the difference between the risks assumed to make money and the risks necessary to protect the fruits of their labors. Two notorious offenders are independent oil producers and real estate developers. Typically they return all of the product of their occupational risk to still more occupational risk activity. That is, the oilman continues to take production from prior oil successes and use it for development or exploration for more oil and gas. Similarly, the real estate developer will continue to make investments in real estate with proceeds of prior successes in real estate. This is acceptable during periods in which the individual continues to be active and productive and is able to replace his reserves. But, at some point, both individuals must begin to take at least a part of what is owned and start substituting financial assets, such as bonds or stocks, for hard assets (hard assets, in this example, being oil and real estate). The ultimate object is to diversify into financial assets (financial assets being investments) which will protect the values and produce a passive income. It is important to remember the financial life cycle dictates that we must all sooner or later substitute passive income for occupational, vocational or professional income. An orderly transition from our vocational activity and the attendant risks into investments producing passive income is a necessary metamorphosis as one progresses through the financial cycle. (Examples of passive income-producing assets include bonds, CD's, dividend-paying common stocks and money market funds.)

Various occupational (accumulation) risks and hazards are not a subject of this book. I mention them only to distinguish clearly between the risks taken to create capital and risks taken in connection with our investments. Investment risks are the various risks assumed during the employment of capital, to protect capital and to create a return on capital satisfying the purpose for accumulating capital in the first place. It is simpler to define investment risks by dividing them into five components: business risk, market risk, purchasing power risk, interest rate risk and political risk.

Business Risk

This risk is the one to which we most often refer when talking about investment risk. It occurs when there is a decline in value or earning power which ultimately reduces an investment's ability to pay interest or dividends or compromises the ability of an investment to pay its obligation such as a bond or a note at its expiration date. A drop in the intrinsic value of the investment or the inability of the obligator of the investment to perform are typical examples of loss resulting from the business risk.

The stock market provides classic examples of business risks. Consider a public utility when it suddenly cuts its dividend. Public Service Company of Indiana (PSI) had been paying a quarterly dividend of more than 70¢. Effective January 1984, the dividend was reduced to 25¢ per quarter. Before the reduction PSI's shares had been commanding a price of $25. Immediately after announcing the lower dividend payment the market price fell to the $8 range. PSI was the same company with the same assets yet suddenly the market values of its shares were reduced by 60%, evidence of the ever-present *business risk* in our investments.

Market Risk

The market risk occurs when there is a change in the market psychology even though the intrinsic value of the investment remains unchanged. The obligator's ability to pay the dividend or interest or meet the payment of the note or obligation of maturity remains strong, and that's a positive factor. But the market psychology may have changed causing the price of the investment or security to decline irrespective of fundamental changes in the earning power or capability of the investment.

An example of the uncertainties of market risk is found in the way bond prices tend to fluctuate contrary to fact and reason, even contrary to logic in some instances. Interest on bonds is superior to dividends on common stock; however, it's interesting to note that many times when a corporation's common stock price falls due to reduced earnings or a cut in dividends, the price of the corporation's bonds tend to also fall. There's no logical justification involved, merely a perception in the market. I recall that when a major airline recently encountered highly publicized difficulties in their negotiations with various labor unions and it looked as if a strike were imminent, the common stock fell by 30%. At the same time the price of the airline's bonds fell also. The bonds were adequately secured by aircraft. So what if the pilots went out on strike? The note payments would still have to be made or else the trustee would take possession of the planes and sell them to other airlines. The bonds were *very well* secured by planes which were in demand. In this instance there was absolutely no reason for bond prices to follow the fate of the common stock— but it occurred just the same. Ultimately the price of the bonds went back to former levels—and then even much higher—within a brief period of time. Obviously the market woke up to the facts. Market risk can be confusing and frustrating because markets are made by human beings. Enough said.

Purchasing Power Risk

The purchasing power risk is one with which we have become more familiar over the last decade or so. A change in general price levels can materially affect the purchasing power of a given investment. A rise in consumer prices, which reduces the buying power of income and principal, will alter the intrinsic value of an investment.

Consider investment in apartments as an example of purchasing power risk. Assume an investor expects to earn 10% on his investments, based on the anticipated return from other investments available at the time with a similar degree of risk. The investor elects to put his money into apartments and calculates the price he is willing to pay for a given property based on a 10% expected return. For example, a $100,000 property yielding an annual net return of $10,000, or 10%, will likely fit into the investor's risk range, depending on his point of view regarding risk/reward. However, if conditions change and the investing community is willing to accept a return of 5% the investor will likely be able to sell his property for $200,000. (Assuming the profit remains constant at $10,000 per year the same property based on its new value of $200,000 will yield 5%.) But purchasing power risk is a double-edged instrument. If interest rates trend upward the value of the property will decline or the investor will find it necessary to increase rents in order to bring the anticipated yield up to competitive levels. Unfortunately an investor is powerless and cannot control the CPI (Consumer Price Index). At best he can try to guess which way prices are *likely* to go and invest accordingly.

Interest Rate Risk

This is a risk which is too often overlooked by many people. A rise in interest rates will tend to depress the price of bonds, notes, CD's, treasury bills and other forms of fixed income investments. These are called *interest sensitive* investments—and for good reason. Conversely, a decrease in interest rates normally increases the price or value of fixed income investments. The interest rate risk has been clearly shown in recent years to be very volatile and will materially affect the value of a particular investment at any given time. While most fixed income investments pay the face value at maturity, the value of the investment may vary substantially due to changes in interest rates during the investment's lifetime. In the case of CD's, for example, severe penalties are imposed if the investment is sold or redeemed before maturity.

Political Risk

Changes in political activity and the resulting changes in wage and price control, tax increases or decreases, changes in tariffs and subsidy policies, and changes in political psychology are examples of political risks. Variations in the financial strength of governmental entities or changes in political attitudes in the contemporary political environment will materially add to or detract from other investment risks. Political risks can force changes in values irrespective of the other four risks discussed.

At this writing interest received from municipal bonds is income tax exempt. When "taxable" interest rates are in the 10% to 12% range, tax-free municipal bonds sell at yields in the range of 7%. An investor in the 50% tax bracket expects a tax-free investment to produce a return approximately 50% *greater* than what would be anticipated from a taxable investment. However, buying a municipal bond today *at any yield* entails certain political risks. This is true because Congress continues debating the possibility of *removing* the tax-exempt advantage in municipal bonds. Today's top-tax-bracket investor buying a 7% municipal bond in anticipation of receiving interest tax-free, thus earning an effective yield of 14%, may later discover that due to changes in tax laws he must pay tax on the interest. Instead of an effective yield (after tax, that is) of 14%, the investor is now paying income tax on the paltry 7% interest—obviously quite a large difference. Therefore, the market value of his 7% bonds will suddenly and severely decrease.

Investing in real estate located in the path of what is expected to be a new highway involves political risk. What if the county or state government decides *not* to build the highway or *changes* the direction of the proposed right of way? In such cases the political risk has proven to be costly to the investor.

To cope with the various investment risks it is wise to consider that certain types of investment hedges are available. They may protect against the various risks, some more adequately than others, though none are perfect or fool proof. You should, therefore, think of your investments as being media through which you make commitments of your discretionary dollars to hedge against various risks and thereby protect your captial while at the same time attempting to provide an adequate return on your commitments. Investment media may be broken down into categories of indirect investments and direct investments. (Chart 7.2)

Indirect investments (common stock, preferred stock, corporate bonds, etc.) are often referred to as liquid investments while *direct* investments (real estate, collectibles, etc.) are less liquid. Investments in syndications and partnerships, most commonly referred to as tax shelters, are often less liquid than stocks or bonds to the extent the individual investor is unable to determine when the property involved should or will be sold. Timing of investment decisions often makes the difference between gain and loss.

Equity investments, as exemplified in common stock and real property, provide inherent hedges against the purchasing power risk because their values tend to track the cost of living more directly than many forms of investment. Stocks and real estate provide protection against most interest rate risks—not so with most preferred stocks, corporate bonds, government bonds and municipal bonds. While there are no perfect investments to hedge against all the

Investment Media

Indirect
  Common Stock

  Preferred Stock

  Corporate Bonds

  Municipal Bonds

  Government Debt Obligations

  Mutual Funds

  Money Market Instruments

Direct
  Real Property

  Collectibles ("Non-Debaseable"; Scarcity)

  Tangible Property

CHART 7.2

risks, different media should be employed to provide a satisfactory balance between risk and reward.

In determining your own personal investment posture Chart 7.3 should be helpful. First, you should provide, as suggested in Chapter Four, adequate liquidity reserves aside from your investments. Then, with a view toward the amounts you have remaining available for investments, consider how much of those funds should be *liquid* at any given time. That is, how much of the total amount do you have available for investments in the form of cash or cash-equivalents? I refer to certificates of deposit, treasury bills, money market funds or similar instruments. Also the *cash* portion of your thrift and profit sharing or 401K plan should not be overlooked. How much of your total position should be in *fixed income* investments, long-term interest-bearing securities such as corporate, government, municipal bonds, notes receivable and the fixed income of your thrift, profit sharing plan or 401K plan? What portion of your total investment capital should be in equities: publicly traded stocks, restricted or closely held stocks, and investment real estate? Determining the correct and best answers requires a careful study of your total objectives and your perception of many outside factors. The amount in the equities portion of your total investment posture, for example, varies with economic conditions. Improving economic conditions, inflationary pressures and/or lower interest rate periods should attract your attention to a greater commitment to equity investment. Higher interest rates, lowering periods of inflation or even disinflation, should cause your attention to become focused on possible increased commitments to *fixed income* investments. When it is difficult to determine the movement of either, build *cash* reserves. It's wise to sit on the sidelines with a wait-and-see attitude in uncertain times. Keep funds invested in short-term (less than one-year maturity) instruments so you can begin to move either into fixed income or equity investments as market conditions become clear. Change your investment posture by keeping in step with social, economic and political changes. Change must become a critical tactic in your overall personal financial and investment strategy. These changes are more profound in producing satisfying investment results through the selection of individual investment media. In my judgment, without a strategy you are simply practicing trial-and-error (Some say trial *by* error!) investment tactics which, though sometimes adequate in the short run, will not produce a satisfactory long-term investment result. Protection of your investment capital can be best obtained by evolving a strategy in selecting investment media consistent with your overall financial strategy. Seek a predetermined form of investment when shifting from *fixed income* to *equities* investment on a percentage basis. Having determined the options before the investment is made, you will likely become satisfied with your investment results as the pre-selected investment will probably fit nicely into the overall strategy. The opposite occurs when one simply selects another approach at the last minute. These unsatisfactory selections are usually picked as a result of a hot tip or an impulsive reaction to sales effort. That's no way to manage investments.

Overall Investment Posture

Personal Liquidity Reserves (Not Investments)

Investment Liquidity Reserves (Cash Or Cash Equivalent)

- Cash
- Certificates Of Deposit
- Money Market Funds Or Instruments
- Qualified Plan Liquidity (Thrift)

Fixed Income (Long Term Interest Bearing)

- Bonds
- Notes Receivable
- Qualified Plan Fixed Income Accounts (Thrift)

Equities

- Publicly Traded Stocks
- Restricted Or Closely-Held Stocks
- Investment Real Estate
- Qualified Plan Equity Accounts (Thrift)
- Stock Options
- Direct Assets

CHART 7.3

Within the *equities* portion of your investment picture your concentration should be given to types of investments which have been carefully and cautiously considered. Again, diversification within the investment media is important. For example, in a common stock area you should be examining the percentages of your total portfolio in different economic classifications of operating companies. Consider economic scenarios such as companies engaged in consumer goods and services versus consumer cyclical goods and services or credit-sensitive industries like banks and insurance companies. Which shows greater promise now and for the foreseeable future? Capital goods industries should be weighed and considered carefully in terms of movement from one industrial group to another within the equity classification of common stocks. Which industrial group indicates greater investment opportunities? Similarly, within the fixed-income area your bond maturity dates should be staggered so that all of your bonds do not come due at the same time. Capital returning to you should be hedged against severe changes in interest rates. By the same token, your credits, whether the issuing obligator is government or corporate, should be varied and staggered so that all of your risk is not with one borrower or on a single time table. In the case of municipal bonds, you should spread your risk among various parts of the country so that a severe recession, depression or decline in economic activity in one part of the country will not play havoc with your overall bond portfolio.

My advice to clients is to develop a municipal bond portfolio with carefully built-in hedges. First hedge geographically. Purchase general obligation bonds located in various parts of the United States. Don't put all your bond dollars in a single market. If the economy in one sector becomes soft or even craters, the bonds in stronger parts of the country will serve to off-set the troubled ones. Next, spread the maturities so the bonds mature in two-year increments over a period of about 15 years. This acts as a hedge against being locked into maturities which are too long and, by the same token, being too heavily committed to short-term rates. The highest quality bonds generate smaller yields while more risky bonds offer higher rewards. By developing a blending of selected bonds you may attain a reasonably attractive, "above-average," yield while maintaining a quality portfolio.

Convertible bonds should be considered for your portfolio. These are instruments with special provisions whereby a bondholder may exchange the bond for shares of common stock at a stated price. If the common stock price climbs above the "striking price" the bond automatically gains an increased value—call it a kicker, if you like. Convertibles enable a bondholder to have security, plus an opportunity for a possible windfall if the common stock goes through the ceiling. Bonds are said by some to be boring. They don't have to be. In fact, bonds can be rather interesting.

In evaluating your investment results, after considering the five risks of investments I have discussed, you should develop a composite rate of return so you can measure each investment relative to alternate media. By composite

Composite Return On Investments

Current Return + Appreciation = Total Return

Example: Assumes 50% Marginal Income Tax
Bracket and 20% Effective Capital Gains Tax

# Shares	Cost Per Share	Dividend Per Share	Appreciation In One Year
100	$70	$6	$10

Dividend Yield		$ 600
Appreciation		1,000
Gross Return		$1,600
Less Taxes		(500)
Net After Tax Return		$1,100

Net Return		Initial Investment		% Return On Investment
$1,100	÷	$7,000	=	15.7%

CHART 7.4

102

Tax Exempt Yield Equivalent To Taxable Yield

Yield	35% Taxpayer	50% Taxpayer
4%	6.1	8.0
6%	9.2	12.0
8%	12.3	16.0
10%	15.4	20.0
12%	18.5	24.0

CHART 7.5

return I refer to the total of the current return plus the appreciation occurring in any given year. Assuming you are in a 50% marginal income tax bracket and a 20% effective capital gains tax rate applies, in this instance your total net return is $1,100. If you bought 100 shares of stock at a cost of $70 per share, and the stock pays $6 a year in dividends, and the shares appreciated $10 per share by the end of the first year, the net result is shown in Chart 7.4. Your dividends would total $600, your appreciation $1,000 less $500 for income tax, leaving a total after-tax return of $1,100. The $1,100 after-tax yield divided by the $7,000 initial investment equals a 15.7% total net return on the investment. Had the value of the stock declined during the year, the return on investment obviously would have been adversely affected. In considering your total return on your investment, always be mindful of your tax position. At this writing interest received on state and municipal bond issues, for example, is exempt from federal income tax. Chart 7.5 shows the tax-exempt yield equivalent to the taxable yield for a 35% and a 50% taxpayer. For example, a taxpayer in the 35% bracket would have to buy a taxable bond or investment yielding at least 15.4% if the taxpayer is to net, after tax, the same 10% afforded through a tax-free municipal bond priced to yield 10%. Obviously, for a 50% taxpayer a 20% taxable investment would provide the same income as a 10% tax-free bond.

Tax-Advantaged Investments
Versus Tax Shelters

I distinguish between tax shelters and tax-advantaged investments as follows (Chart 7.6): *Tax shelters* are those kinds of commitments wherein the tax advantages or deductions constitute the main purpose of the commitment. *Tax-advantaged investments* are those wherein the economic or business purpose is the primary consideration while the tax savings is a convenient by-product. Generally, one should make maximum use of tax-advantaged investments and avoid tax-shelter investments. This should be in keeping with investment decisions based *first* on personal objectives; *second,* on good economic and business decisions; and *third,* on tax considerations. (Chart 7.7) But, remember, *always* in that order. Chart 7.8 illustrates a list of tax-advantaged investments. Chart 7.9 illustrates their values. Many of these are frequently overlooked by the average investor. However, these investments should be considered in most personal and financial strategies. The general area of the employer benefit program affords many advantages in the form of tax-advantaged investment opportunities. The contributions often are deductible or pre-taxed. The accumulations in the plans are tax free, and the distributions from tax advantaged plans afford many benefits over other forms of investments. Similarly, your investments in IRA's, Keoghs and other forms of self-employment retirement programs provide greater tax savings than the usual non-advantaged investments.

"Tax-Advantaged Investments"
vs.
Tax Shelters

- Tax Benefits Are By-Products Of An "Investment" Or Arrangement Based On Personal Factors Or Economic Merit

- Tax Benefits Are The Primary Rationale For The "Investment" Or Arrangement

CHART 7.6

105

Evaluation Of Tax-Advantaged Investment For You

- **Personal Appropriateness**
  Correlation To Your Other Investments
  Non-Liquidability Tolerance

- **Economic Merit**
  Sound Financial Basis
  Reasonable Risks For Return

- **Tax Benefits**
  Value Of Deductions And Credits
  Backlash: Recapture, Preference,
  Deduction Denial

CHART 7.7

"Tax-Advantaged Investments"

- Qualified Benefit Plans (Thrift, IRA, Keogh, 401K)

- Mortgaged Homestead (Dual Purpose: Personal And Investment)

- Leveraged Stock Option Exercise And Hold Strategy

- Reversionary Trust

- Gifts Of Appreciated Property (Charitable, Personal)

- Tax-Exempt Debt Instruments (Municipal Bonds, Project Notes)

- Alternative Disposition Methods To Simple Sale (Corporate, Charitable)

CHART 7.8

107

"Tax-Advantaged Investment" Axioms

- Liquidability And Tax Benefits Are Inversely Related

- "At-Risk-Rules" Limit Deductions To Your Real Economic Risk, Except For Leveraged Real Estate

- Tax Avoidance Schemes Are Virtually Non-Existent

- Deferral Of Tax Can Be A Reasonable Result

- Conversion Of The Taxable Character Of Income (Ordinary To Capital Gains) Can be A Reasonable Result

The Ultimate Outcome Of A "Tax Shelter" Investment Depends On The Economic Merits Of The Investment

CHART 7.9

108

In considering commitments to tax shelters, syndications or partnerships, review the points listed in Chart 7.10. The track record of the general partner must be thoroughly investigated with respect to past results and not solely from the standpoint of the tax deductibility of the shelter. Be aware of *all* the fees and charges and other costs which must be paid. Face it; you, the investor, will be doing the paying. The track record of the general partner and his proven investment results cannot be investigated too thoroughly by the prospective investor.

When one takes advantage of the opportunities afforded today through employer benefit plans, internal business benefit programs, professional organization programs, together with Keoghs and IRA's as well as making wise use of credit in home financing and investment and consumer credit, the individual will have availed himself of *the most meaningful forms of tax reduction.* On the other hand, one may make excessive commitments to nonliquid forms of investment, such as in partnerships and syndications, which tie up credit, reduce cash flow and impair liquidity. These "investments" generally provide additional revenues for attorneys and accountants. The IRS has a way of closely examining tax returns of *all* the participants. The IRS is looking for suitability of deductions "afforded" by the typical tax shelter. Today's newspapers inform us regularly of the fates of many hapless "investors" who have selected questionable tax shelters for their financial plans. Some have been required to pay substantial penalties over and above the payment of the taxes! My advice regarding syndications and partnerships is, in a word, "*caution.*"

It should also be kept in mind that many taxpayers, as I have learned from experience, are not in as high effective tax brackets as they think. Carefully examine your latest return and calculate the percent of the tax you paid relative to your income. You will probably find the percentage of income paid in taxes to be *less* than you expected. A careful consideration of your commitments to tax-reduction schemes and methods should result from this simple, yet effective, self-examination.

In developing your personal investment strategy as part of your overall financial planning be certain you avoid the perils of procrastination. (Chart 7.11) Procrastination manifests itself in missed investment opportunities, to name but one evil of putting off important financial decisions. You simply fail to get around to making a commitment to something that should have been an important part of your overall strategy. Lost time equals lost money. You will not like the results of inappropriate timing and retaining wrong investments too long. Failure to minimize losses or failure to recognize gains usually results from carelessness or simple procrastination. Sometimes we blame oversight.

My experience indicates we are too often inclined to stay with our winners because they have been productive for us, but at the same time our ego often prevents us from recognizing our losses. If an investment has not per-

Evaluation Of A Specific Tax-Advantaged Investment

Reputation of Principals
- Syndicator Profit Not Tied to Deal Success
- Conflicts of Interest
- Front End Fees
- Track Record
- Expertise

Economic Viability
- Estimated Returns Relative to Industry Standards
- Error Margin Allowances
- Basic Assumption
- Consultation with Objective Experts

CHART 7.10

110

Avoid Perils Of Procrastination

- **Missed Investment Opportunities**

- **Effects of Inappropriate Timing**
  - **Retaining Investments too Long**
  - **Failure to Minimize Losses**
  - **Failure to Recognize Gains**

- **Lost Tax Savings Opportunities / Alternatives**

- **Inefficient Use of Resources**

- **Failure to Meet Personal Objectives**

CHART 7.11

111

formed as well as we hoped yet remains a good one in our judgment, we should consider adding more shares at the lower cost. Many investors refer to this as *averaging down.* The same is true of investments which are doing as well or better than expected. The professionals call it *averaging up,* and the system has been known to make many investors very rich. Timing is everything in investing, and subjective ties to investments should be discarded in favor of objective evaluation—not only when we first make the commitment but on a recurring basis as well. A wise employer systematically and periodically reviews and appraises his employees. A wise investor does likewise with his investments. Occasionally an investment must be fired.

Of the three decisions involved in investment—buying, selling and retaining—you should keep in mind that the retain decision is just as much an investment decision as either the buy or the sell. Too often we procrastinate and lose tax-savings opportunities or other potential gains by simply not making a timely decision. NO decision is just as much a decision as a good choice or a bad one. We also let procrastination prolong inefficient uses of our resources, i.e., leaving excess cash in a checking account, a NOW account or a low-yielding investment. Procrastination generally contributes to a failure to meet our personal financial objectives.

As you go about deploying or re-deploying your capital for investment purposes, (1) Remember the Historical Perspective of the basic watershed period the economy is undergoing and the changes taking place in the world as well as our nation. (2) Note changes in Moreism. Consider that Moreism may no longer be in vogue as it once was. Remember that inflation, excessive government expenditure and heavy debt may not provide for upward mobility in income and/or assets simply due to the socio-economic environment. (3) Recognize the Hourglass Scenario of the financial life cycle and precisely where you presently find yourself. (4) Be Aware of Group Decision-Making in your personal financial strategy. (Chart 7.12)

Don't delay developing your financial strategy. Avoid the perils, pitfalls and costs of procrastination. (See the following Comments for an example of an exception to this rule.) To accumulate, concentrate on the occupational risk, the vocational risk, and the professional risk and deal only in media you know a great deal about. Diversify later through an understanding of and a hedge against the investment risks to protect your money and make it productive. When you have done these, you deserve a great deal.

A SAD BUT TRUE COMMENTARY

The former chairman of the board of a major company came to see me not too long ago. He had been retired almost five years. He told me he had $200,000.00 in gold Krugerrands in his IRA rollover account! An IRA rollover is an account that accumulates income tax-free, and since the Kruger-

Thoughts To Remember

- Remember Historical "PERSPECTIVE"

- Note Changes In "MOREISM"

- Recognize The "HOURGLASS" Scenario And Where You Are

- Be Aware Of "GROUP" Decision Making

CHART 7.12

113

rands produce no income the tax-free advantage of the IRA rollover was completely lost with this type of foolish investment.

Another client, a $450,000-base-salaried executive, did not know that publicly traded bonds could be sold prior to their maturity date! Another individual who had recently sold his business for a gain of several million dollars did not know that changing interest rates can cause a variation in bond prices or that bond prices vary with general interest rates.

Recently another retiree of a major company came to see me. This was some three years after his retirement. He had been advised—poorly, I might add—to take the funds from his benefit plans, both pension and thrift, in a lump sum. He had paid taxes on the proceeds, foregoing the option of the 10-year averaging or an IRA rollover. He had been advised, "sold" is more accurate, tax-deferred annuities which he could have had under his benefit plans without having taken a lump sum and having paid all those taxes! He also had been sold gold and silver as *investments* as well as some dubious *gold mining* stocks. Next he had been put into three real estate tax shelters creating a $300,000 debt on his financial statement! This, by the way, was the largest debt this poor soul had ever incurred in his life. He had recently had a cash call on one of his so-called tax shelters. I wondered what would have been his status if one or two of the other "shelters" had also turned into cash calls. He told me he had not fully understood the tax shelters, which was the classic understatement of the year. The "guaranteed" interest rate under his tax-deferred annuity had already dropped by over three hundred basis points. He told me he did not know it was possible for such a thing to happen.

This man's net worth had been *rearranged* for the benefit, in my judgment, of some salespeople—certainly not for the benefit of the retiree. This weird and tragic example of *misplanning* casts a long dark question mark over the sound advice in Chart 7.11. In this sad case, procrastination would have been a million-dollar *advantage*.

Chapter Eight

PERSONAL, EMPLOYER AND GOVERNMENT BENEFITS

In creating and evaluating your personal financial strategy one of the most important elements, and the least understood and most often overlooked, are the various benefit programs. Within the typical benefit programs, an employee usually has a great deal of financial planning already in place. This is certainly true when he takes full advantage of them. First, however, the employee must have a clear understanding of the programs and their many benefits. There are basically three types of benefits with which we should be familiar. We shall consider the use of them in an appropriate format within the personal financial strategy. First let's review all three: private programs, employer programs and government programs.

PRIVATE PROGRAMS

In recent years private programs have become increasingly popular thanks to new and expanded provisions made available by various acts of Congress. The most important of the private programs are the individual retirement accounts (IRA) and the self-employed retirement accounts (Keogh).

Under current law an employed or working individual may contribute $2,000 a year to an individual retirement account plus an added $250 if the taxpayer has a non-income-producing spouse. If, however, the spouse is also incoming-producing an additional $2,000 may be contributed making a total annual contribution of $4,000 for a two-income family. The amount contributed to the IRA is deducted before taxes are calculated. The entire IRA contribution comes "off the top," to use a popular accounting phrase. In addition, the amount of the IRA's earnings is exempt from federal income taxation. The IRA may be withdrawn any time after the taxpayer reaches 59 years 6 months of age and *must* be withdrawn beginning at age 70 years 6 months. Withdrawals may be over the actuarial life expectancy of the IRA owner at the time the withdrawals begin. The withdrawals are subject to the IRA owner's individual income tax bracket at the time of withdrawal. Chart 8.1 shows the accumulation potential of a typical IRA account for people at various ages and exemplifies the amount of accumulation possible on a compound tax-free interest basis. The assumption here is that the IRA account earns 8% over its life and the annual contributions are made under present law. Most experts agree Congress will probably increase the maximum contributions allowable thus making IRA's even more attractive. It's difficult to believe, yet true, that more than 70% of all taxpayers eligible for IRA's have *not* taken advantage of this excellent tax break.

The fact that the majority of Americans are still sitting on the IRA sidelines amazes me. To further compound the mystery consider the case of the prospective client who told me the reason he had not started an IRA: "I am putting $2,000 a year into a real estate tax shelter and I don't have any money left over for an IRA." An IRA is the world's best tax shelter and here's a self-proclaimed sophisticated executive who overlooks the obvious while utilizing a dubious and risky method for avoiding and postponing the payment of income taxes. Another IRA mystery is found in the fact that so few people realize they can borrow the $2,000 ($2,250 if married to a non-working spouse or $4,000 for a two-income family) annual contribution. If a taxpayer is short of funds he may simply go to a bank and borrow the money. The interest paid on the loan is deductible while the funds contributed into the IRA reduce the current tax burden. The sooner the money is at work in an IRA the sooner the magic of tax-free compounding goes to work. IRA's are so simple it literally boggles many minds.

The self-employed retirement account (commonly known as the Keogh) has withdrawal provisions similar to the individual retirement account. However, the amount which may be contributed through a defined-contribution Keogh plan is equal to as much as 15% of the self-employed's income with a maximum of $30,000 per year. Funds in a Keogh account, also known as an HR–10 account, earn tax-free income. Ordinary income tax rates prevail when withdrawals are made either optionally at age 59 years 6 months or mandatorily at 70 years 6 months. Another form of Keogh is known as the Defined Benefit Keogh. This plan makes it possible for professionals or self-employeds to achieve their own personal pension plan. Actuarial determination must be made of the correct amount to be contributed into the plan in order to provide the desired pension at the estimated retirement age. It is extremely important that the self-employed carefully and fully investigate this type of Keogh. Too often the Defined Benefit Keogh is overlooked when selecting an overall benefit plan for the self-employed or professional.

The investment media selected for an IRA or a Keogh, in my judgment, should be kept simple and relatively risk free. Be certain your investments are mainly in assets producing income. One of the greatest values of the private benefit plans is that they generate *tax-free* accumulation. Compounding income in a tax-free account such as an IRA or Keogh will amount to substantial growth. Interest rates as seen on Chart 8.1 certainly prove the "magic" of compound interest over a period of years. Avoid investing assets of a tax-favored plan like an IRA or Keogh in real estate and/or oil and gas properties where depreciation and depletion are important factors in the economics of the investment. They are of little or no value in a tax-free fund such as an IRA or Keogh. Similarly, impotent and sterile types of investments such as gold, silver and other metals have no place in an IRA or Keogh. Concentrate on financial assets producing a reasonable rate of return and those you anticipate will increase over a period of years. Capital gains accrue in IRA and Keogh plans without tax consequence. Compound interest and income accretion factors plus capital gains will produce a substantial growth and enhancement of your tax-advantaged retirement plans.

Keogh plans have been around since the mid–1960's. IRA's are a newer invention. Nevertheless, even during the short periods of time involved, I have witnessed phenomenal growth in both plans. I have clients who presently have more than $500,000 in their Keogh plans. In some cases these funds were invested in stocks which have enjoyed unusually outstanding success. In one case the individual parlayed his Keogh through astute commodity trading, something I advise against. A client of mine has his IRA in a self-directed "mutual fund" and has been able to double his money every eighteen months. He's a very successful stock picker with an uncanny sense of timing. I advise against this strategy unless, of course, you are as successful in the market as this particular client. When one is able to turn money at accelerated rates and do it without the disadvantage of taxation, it's truly amazing how rapidly one may enhance retirement funds. These IRA and Keogh pensioners are some of the people constituting the universe I have so often mentioned: the millions who will inherit billions. Keoghs and IRA's will easily amount to more than a million dollars for a great many astute planners retiring before the end of the decade. People who took advantage of these tax-favored laws from the time they first became available will be retiring in the 1990's and beyond with $2 and $3 million in their funds (assuming they are age 59 years six months at the time). Even persons who put their Keogh and IRA money into banks or savings and loans will find that tax-free compounding works like magic. Those who put in the *maximum* amount allowed and at the *earliest* possible dates will find their retirement fund will likely be $100,000 or more *larger*

Individual Retirement Account
Earning 8%

Total Annual Contribution	Balance With Contributions From Age 25 To Age	
	59 1/2	70 1/2
$2,250	$372,015	$ 904,857
$4,000	$661,360	$1,608,635

CHART 8.1

118

than those funds belonging to procrastinating taxpayers in the habit of making their contributions closer to annual deadlines. Remember, when compounding interest time is of the essence.

I have many clients who are now retired and enjoying the fruits of their Keogh plans. Some are drawing comfortable incomes from their plans while the fund itself continues to grow faster than the retiree makes his withdrawals. They'll never outlive their incomes.

EMPLOYER BENEFIT PLANS

This is perhaps the most important area of accumulation for most citizens of the United States. Employer benefit plans have expanded rapidly all across this great nation, particularly since World War II. When one thinks of employer compensation programs in the aggregate, it is important to understand how they work in tandem with other investments and cash-flow planning as well as with insurance requirements. There are five basic methods of compensation under a typical employer benefit arrangement: direct, replacement (life insurance and disability income), retirement, protective (health and medical) and capital.

Direct Compensation

This is the cash, or in some instances stock payments, one receives providing for one's basic lifestyle. (Chart 8.2) The most important and best known components, of course, are salary and bonus. These are, in many instances, the most important elements of cash-flow, and as you develop a cash-flow plan, salary and bonus will likely prove to be the major contributors. Direct compensation is also your most important source of cash for purposes of meeting debt obligations, paying insurance premiums, providing for taxes and creating adequate depreciation reserves. Direct compensation also enables a worker to match employer benefit contribution requirements as well as basic monthly expense budgets of both fixed and variable expenses. Allocation of your salary and bonus among those elements in your personal financial life will produce the most desirable utilization of your overall private employer and government benefits.

Replacement Compensation

The next component of your compensation program is that of replacement compensation. (Chart 8.3) These programs are designed to provide protection to replace income if and when it is cut off for any reason. They include life insurance and disability income protection.

Life insurance replaces income loss due to death of the insured. This is accomplished, as a rule, through group life insurance programs provided by

Direct Compensation

Cash/Stock Payments to Provide for a Certain Standard of Living

Components

- Salary

- Bonus

CHART 8.2

120

Replacement Compensation

Protection To Replace An Executive's Income When Cut Off For Any Reason

Components

Death

- Life Insurance

(Basic and Supplemental)

- Accidental Life Insurance

Disability

- Short-Term Coverage

- Permanent Coverage

Retirement

- Pension

CHART 8.3

121

the employer. Often employer programs provide basic amounts of death benefits while the employee is allowed to purchase supplemental amounts at bargain-basement group rates negotiated by the employer. There are additional death benefits provided by many employers for accidental death. Many even allow added accidental death coverage while traveling on business. These basic and accidental insurance plans should be considered when purchasing additional coverage outside the employer-sponsored programs. Consider carefully the advantages of purchasing supplemental amounts and attractive low rates available through company-sponsored group programs.

Disability income protection is an important element of replacement compensation. Most up-to-date employer benefit plans include short-term coverage. Provisions are made for benefits paid for the first thirty days to six months of disability followed by long-term benefits paid on a permanent-coverage basis after short-term income benefits are exhausted. Be sure you understand the terms and amounts available in the event of both short-term as well as permanent disability. The amounts provided under your employer benefit plan should then be coordinated with the amounts of disability insurance purchased individually. Make certain you have adequate amounts of income replacement protection required in your family's particular situation. Do not rely totally on an employer-sponsored benefit program to provide the necessary amounts of disability income protection. You may change jobs or the employer may drop or reduce the coverage. In either case, you will acquire a high degree of satisfaction and peace of mind knowing you *own* your own coverage—come what may.

An important additional replacement compensation program provided by your employer is a sound retirement plan. This may be a pension plan or some kind of a defined benefit plan. You must understand all options available to you as well as the amount of retirement benefit you will receive at normal or early retirement.

Most pension plans provided by an employer allow for optional settlements. Some provide a pension of a certain amount for life with no survivor benefit to your spouse or other family members. Other options enable you to take a lower pension during your life with the same amount or a fractional amount available to your spouse should you die before your spouse. There is also an *annuity-certain* option found in many retirement programs wherein you may elect to receive a lesser amount but receive that specified monthly income for a set number of years such as ten or twenty years after retirement. This insures that your family will receive a specific amount regardless of how long—or how short a period—you and/or your spouse may live.

Under many programs today, lump sum settlement is available through retirement plans. This allows you to take the pension in annuity form or take a lump sum, pay income tax on it or roll it over to an IRA account and thereby increase your total investment capital subject to IRA-rollover provisions. The IRA rollover is discussed more completely in Chapter 10. But suffice it to say, there are many valuable options under most employer-sponsored pension plans. Take the time necessary to learn all about these valuable plans and their options. Be certain you recognize them and properly integrate them into your personal financial plan.

Protective Compensation

Protective compensation is another very important employer benefit. (Chart 8.4) This type of compensation provides protection for you and your family against the risk of increased expenses due to unpredictable events. Basic components involve health care coverage, major medical, and dental insurance. Provisions for childbirth and mental illness are also occasionally included. It is important to understand the components of protective compensation benefits provided by your employer. Knowing the details of these benefits enables you to make adequate provision for any deficiencies you find in these programs through private plans. By the acquisition of supplemental insurance programs and/or the provision of additional cash-flow accruals in your personal cash management system, you will be able to compensate for major unpredictable catastrophic events not adequately provided for through employer benefit programs.

Capital Compensation

Many modern employer benefit programs include what I identify as capital compensation benefits. The basic components of these programs are savings plans, thrift plans, profit-sharing plans and salary-deferral programs. (Chart 8.5) Another important component available for senior management and executives are options to purchase stock in the employer company. Popular new stock ownership plans, known as ESOP's, are now available in some employer programs. Each of these capital compensation plans is designed to provide an orderly method for accumulation of employee capital. Income and appreciation from investments in these programs may be used for major financial commitments such as financing an education, acquiring a second home, supplementing retirement benefits and/or accumulating an estate for purposes of passing substantial assets to future generations. These are excellent vehicles for providing additional self-sufficiency in the preservation stage of one's life cycle. Carefully review the amounts being contributed on your behalf into these programs, including the basic provisions and options. Be certain to accurately determine what amounts, if any, you will contribute to the plans. Not all plans, however, allow for employee contributions. The amounts contributed to these programs should be looked upon as an integral part of your

Protective Compensation

Protection Against The Risk of a Short–Term Drain on an Executive's Income From Unpredictable Events

Components

- Basic Health Care Coverage

- Major Medical

- Dental

CHART 8.4

Capital Compensation

Income And Appreciation From Investments May Aid In

- Financing Educations, Vacation Homes
- Supplementing Retirement
- Passing Assets To Next Generation

Components

- Savings Plan
- Stock Options
- Employee Stock Ownership Plan (ESOP)

CHART 8.5

overall investment programs used in cash management system calculations. Capital compensation is to be taken into account when determining vocational-to-passive income ratios needed as one progresses through the financial life cycle.

Charts 8.6, 8.7 and 8.8 illustrate an interesting series of accruals in the salary deferral program commonly known as the 401K. The charts show the difference between a contribution to the pre-tax 401K versus a *taxable* savings plan. You can readily see the contributions provide interesting and substantial accumulations, particularly if matching funds, as illustrated, are provided by the employer. In many instances, matching funds are provided.

Salary Deferral Program (401 K)
Investment Potential

After–Tax Annual Contribution	Company Matching	Total Annual Contribution	Balance With Contribution From Age 30 to Age	
			59 1/2	65
$4,000	$4,000	$8,000	$950,833	$1,529,255

Pre–Tax Annual Contribution	Company Matching	Total Annual Contribution	Balance With Contribution From Age 30 to Age	
			59 1/2	65
$8,000	$8,000	$16,000	$1,901,666	$3,058,510

Notes: Assumes 8% Earnings Compounded Monthly

CHART 8.6

127

Salary Deferral Program (401 K)
Investment Potential

After–Tax Annual Contribution	Company Matching	Total Annual Contribution	Balance With Contribution From Age 40 to Age	
			59 1/2	65
$4,000	$4,000	$8,000	$373,425	$634,018

Pre–Tax Annual Contribution	Company Matching	Total Annual Contribution	Balance With Contribution From Age 40 to Age	
			59 1/2	65
$8,000	$8,000	$16,000	$746,850	$1,268,035

Notes: Assumes 8% Earnings Compounded Monthly

CHART 8.7

Salary Deferral Program (401 K)
Investment Potential

After–Tax Annual Contribution	Company Matching	Total Annual Contribution	Balance With Contribution From Age 50 to Age	
			59 1/2	65
$4,000	$4,000	$8,000	$113,289	$230,692

Pre–Tax Annual Contribution	Company Matching	Total Annual Contribution	Balance With Contribution From Age 50 to Age	
			59 1/2	65
$8,000	$8,000	$16,000	$226,578	$461,384

Notes: Assumes 8% Earnings Compounded Monthly

CHART 8.8

GOVERNMENT BENEFIT PROGRAMS

Take the time necessary to study the benefits available to you under Social Security and Medicare. You should also understand the benefits, if any, available to you under Veterans Administration programs. If you have served in the military of the United States, you are likely eligible for various VA benefits. Government programs provide liberal benefits and can become substantial factors in any personal financial plan. Chart 8.9 shows the types of benefits available under current Social Security law for retirement, disability and survivors. Survivor benefits are outlined in Chart 8.10. Retirement benefits are outlined in Chart 8.11. The disability provisions of Social Security are shown in Chart 8.12 and should be considered as part of the overall disability income protection plans previously discussed. Chart 8.13 illustrates current Medicare benefits.

Veterans Administration programs provide both term and whole life insurance policies at nominal rates. Disability, retirement or handicap provisions are available to eligible veterans for both military related and non-military-related handicaps. You should become familiar with these benefits. They may constitute an important role in your planning consideration and in determining the amounts of life insurance, disability protection and health insurance needed to complete your insurance programs. Death benefits as well as burial provisions are available to most veterans of the various branches of the United States military.

The wise use and the efficient integration of private, employer and government benefit programs into your overall financial strategy cannot be overemphasized. These programs help the astute planner reach his or her financial goals. It is imperative that you develop a clear understanding of all these programs and their applicability to your particular situation. This understanding prepares you to make wise choices and to take appropriate actions under the terms of each of the many plans. Decisions must be coordinated with other financial strategy considerations. Often we find the family's personal financial activity in conflict with choices available to them under various benefit programs. Careful study is called for. Too often careless planners make incorrect assumptions about these benefits. Don't be guilty of building a financial plan on a foundation of sand and assumptions.

Having taken these many and varied plans into account in your overall financial plan, be certain the benefits are not duplicated when analyzing your personal situation. Neither should you assume that these various public and private programs are adequate on their own. You could find yourself overinsured or overprotected in the event of catastrophe. On the other hand, you could be underprotected.

Your situation remains uniquely your own. Relate your individual posture to all of these programs which are applicable. Make necessary fine-tuning adjustments in your personal financial strategy to account for outside benefits.

Government Benefits

Social Security

Three Types of Benefits

- **Retirement Checks**
  - Age 62 reduced
  - Age 65 full

- **Disability Checks**
  - Covers disability
  - Before age 65

- **Survivors Checks**
  - Surviving spouse
  - Age 60 or over
  - Dependents
  - Lump sum death benefit

Benefits based on average yearly earnings under Social Security over period of years.

CHART 8.9

131

Survivor Benefits

- The spouse of a deceased worker at age 65 is eligible to receive tax-free monthly income benefits equal to the full age-65 retirement pension that would have been granted to the deceased worker.

- A widow or widower of any age caring for a child under the age of 16 receives a check equal to 75% of the decedent's full retirement benefit and each unmarried child under the age of 18 can draw a 75% benefit check.

- Social Security provides a $255 lump sum burial benefit at death.

CHART 8.10

132

Retirement Benefits

● At age 65 you are entitled to full retirement benefits under the Social Security program (pension linked to past earnings).

● You may take early retirement at age 62 and collect 80% of the pension you would have received if you had continued working until age 65.

● After retirement, your spouse also qualifies for a pension at age 65, receiving a check equal to 50% of your benefit.

● If you retire at age 65 and have unmarried children under the age of 18, each child is entitled to 50% of your full retirement benefit up to a prescribed maximum.

CHART 8.11

Disability Benefits

- If you become disabled prior to age 65, you may receive tax-free monthly benefits under the Social Security program.

- You are entitled to these benefits after a five month waiting period, if you are unable to engage in any gainful activity. A disabled person is treated, in effect, as a person drawing retirement benefits.

- In addition, your disability may entitle your spouse and children to benefits.

- If you are on disability for two years, you qualify automatically for Medicare benefits regardless of your age.

- The total Social Security payments, combined with state or private insurance disability income, cannot be higher than 80% of your average income before suffering the disability.

CHART 8.12

134

Medicare Benefits

- At age 65 retirement or disability, you are automatically eligible to apply for the Medicare program provided for by Social Security.

- Under this program, basic hospital insurance provides for hospital and related care.

- A supplementary plan (for which a small premium is charged) covers physician's charges and certain other health related services.

CHART 8.13

135

THE MILLIONAIRE WAGE EARNER

The remarkable and marvelous results to be derived from employer benefit plans are now surfacing and becoming clearly evident. Just as in the cases of Keogh and IRA plans, the orderly and systematic accumulation of funds over a period of time, coupled with the magic of compounding interest and eliminating the effect of the tax wringer, is creating a new generation of millionaires—a class of retirees who'll enjoy a special form of freedom.

I was recently working with a local refrigeration repairman who has been working for a large retailer for many years. His employer provides him with a profit sharing plan which has grown to the point where the repairman's share is worth more than $350,000. The plan is continuing to grow nicely thanks to its tax-free accumulations. This man, who is 55 years of age, told me he has never earned more than $25,000 a year. In addition to his company plan he has been building an IRA for the past five years.

Together we calculated that he may retire in approximately five years at an annual income well in excess of his present level of earnings and *never outlive the income*. He will be able to travel and do whatever he desires. As he said, "I'll be free!" Of course, one of his options is to continue working even until he is age 70. If he does so his company benefits and his IRA would keep getting bigger and bigger, making him a bona fide retired millionaire. Not bad for a blue collar worker with less than a high school education. This is an actual example of a completely new dimension of freedom available to every working person. This repairman is wealthy by any standard, and he's getting richer by the day. He anticipates he will receive Social Security retirement benefits along with his company and IRA benefits. However, he *knows* he will be retiring rich and comfortable regardless of the Federal government's plan known as Social Security. That's the kind of freedom every "wealthy" person may look forward to.

Chapter Nine

ESTATE PLANNING

Having accepted the reality and finality of his own mortality, man has long grappled with the realistic yet ever-pressing need for planning for the *eventuality* and *certainty* of death. Think of estate planning as life and death planning. It's positive and potentially profitable activity and one deserving a great deal of time and thought. Execution of a Last Will and Testament is a privilege afforded in the United States and most western countries but not always available to those in other civilizations. The oldest known will is that of Uah, King of Egypt, who in Kahoun, Egypt around 1805 B.C., executed his last will and testament. Most legal authorities today believe his will would stand in any probate, surrogate or county court in the United States should Uah have died last week. Too bad we can't say that much for some modern-day wills.

Julius Caesar gave us the classic case for keeping one's will up-to-date. Julius left an outdated will naming Octavian (who later became Augustus rather than Caesarean), his son by Cleopatra, as his successor. Such was life and death in ancient Rome's fast lane. Rabelais, in 1533 B.C., took a more feudalistic approach in his will when he said, "I have no available property. I owe a great deal. The rest I give to the poor." Henry VIII was granted power to appoint a successor under his will should he have no children, no children to speak of, that is. So the will has served many people to varying degrees of success over many, many centuries. The point is mortal man has been gravely concerned about what happens to his accumulations when he departs this life. Our family and descendants share the same degree of interest in the subject when considering "something may happen" to us. Isn't it interesting how we avoid saying "when we die"? I think the most important caveat here is that it's not an *if* situation we are dealing with, but rather a *when*. Some prefer to say "if he dies," when in reality the meaning is "when he dies." The need for sound estate planning to cope with great exigencies of life and death is imperative for everyone and for every plan. When I say the great exigencies of life, I refer to the following: (1) *Living too long* and becoming unable to care for ourselves or our financial affairs; (2) *Dying too soon* and, therefore, not completing our goals and ambitions; and (3) *Disability* or impairment preventing us from continuing to function in a financially productive manner. Some call this the "living death."

We have available to us the modern legal and financial tools necessary to develop a plan for ourselves and for our families which deal with these three exigencies. No individual and, indeed, no family should be without an up-to-date and comprehensive estate plan.

Fundamental estate planning begins with the recognition of the need for preparation and the execution of your last will and testament. The will is a legally enforceable document directing the disposition of your assets. Everyone should have one, yet millions die each year without a will. The majority of people today still fail to have a properly drawn will in spite of the fact we have the highest ratio of attorneys to the general population in the entire world. It makes one wonder what all those attorneys are doing. Understand that if you do not execute a will, the state in which you live has laws governing intestate (when you die without a will) distribution of your assets. Therefore, in a sense, *everyone* has a will. Some draw their own while others let the state do it for them. You should also remember that your will does not control property held in joint ownership. Similarly, your will does not control properties subject to beneficiary designations, such as life insurance, savings plans at your company, stock-option programs where you have an interest, your employee stock-ownership plan, bonus program, or IRA's and Keoghs with beneficiary designations. These beneficiaries are not controlled by your will and, therefore, you may inadvertently provide disposition of property counterproductive to your original intentions. In effect, many of us have five or six other "wills" if we have not coordinated the beneficiary designation under the various programs which we have. Our overall last will and testament provisions should be drawn with the beneficiary designations in mind.

There are three basic types of wills. The *holographic* will is one made in your own handwriting. It usually does not need witnesses and is readily acceptable for probate in most states. The second type of will is the *nuncupative* will, a verbal will which is usually admitted to probate in most states. This is generally known as a death-bed will, where one verbally expresses his or her wishes as to the disposition of assets. The "will" is made before witnesses who later may testify as to the deceased's testamentary desires. The *standard* will or typewritten will prepared by a qualified attorney and signed before witnesses at the time of execution is, of course, the preferred instrument. One should not plan to leave an estate under either a handwritten or a death-bed nuncupative verbal will. It's tantamount to leaving no will in many instances.

At your death your will is admitted to probate. Probate is the legal process of presenting a will to the court along with proof of the document's validity, the death certificate, the appointment of the executor named in the will, and the confirmation of authority upon the designated executor to settle the estate. When you die with a will wherein the document names an executor, the court will normally appoint the executor who has been designated. When you die with a will but do not name an executor, the court will appoint an administrator with the will annexed, meaning the administrator will be appointed by the court to execute the will subject to the probate court's approval. When you die without a will and your estate requires administration due to the fact there are debts and/or taxes to pay, the court will appoint an administrator. A guardian will be appointed in the event you become incapacitated or non compis mentis (mentally incompetent). The executor and/or the guardian are, in effect, personal representatives carrying out and executing the wishes of the deceased and the management of properties for the duration of the estate settlement. The executor is usually a responsible party such as a competent adult or a bank or trust company who is charged with administering the instructions of the will in compliance with the estates legal obligations.

The typical probate proceedings are as follows: An attorney prepares an application to the court in each state and county in which the deceased owned real estate or held mineral interests at the time of death. The court approves the probate application when it finds that the will presented is truly the Last Will and Testament of the decedent and that the executor is qualified under the laws of that state to act. The executor is then appointed by the court and the executor signs an oath to serve the estate.

The executor's duties are many:

- Determine ownership and take possession of all assets owned by the estate
- Determine and verify all liabilities
- Prepare an evaluation of all assets owned at the date of death
- Provide an inventory evaluation, appraisements and list of claims
- Prepare periodic accounting reports
- Prepare and file appropriate tax returns
- Implement income and estate tax planning strategies
- Make decisions for income distributions for the family
- Distribute from the estate to the beneficiaries as provided in the will.

Unified Transfer Tax Rate Schedule

| If the Amount is: | | Tentative Tax is: | | | |
Over	But Not Over	Tax	+	%	On Excess Over
60,000	80,000	13,000		26	60,000
80,000	100,000	18,200		28	80,000
100,000	150,000	23,800		30	100,000
150,000	250,000	38,800		32	150,000
250,000	500,000	70,800		34	250,000
500,000	750,000	155,800		37	500,000
750,000	1,000,000	248,300		39	750,000
1,000,000	1,250,000	345,800		41	1,000,000
1,250,000	1,500,000	448,300		43	1,250,000
1,500,000	2,000,000	555,800		45	1,500,000
2,000,000	2,500,000	780,800		49	2,000,000
2,500,000	3,000,000	1,025,800		53	2,500,000

CHART 9.1

There are a multitude of taxes involved in settling an estate. The most important are federal, state and gift taxes. In 1977 legislation created a unified transfer tax. As a result of the law, there is no longer a distinction between gifting assets while one is alive and willing assets under a legal will. A unified transfer credit is now available allowing transfer of a specific dollar amount to be acquired against transfers made by gifts while the donor is alive or by transfer under a last will and testament. Of course, there are local and state estate taxes which are enforced on many estates by and in the various states.

You should also be aware that foreign country transfer taxes may be applicable on properties which are owned in those countries. The United States has treaties with various major countries covering foreign taxes, that is, taxes imposed by the foreign governments. Often those treaties do not cover provincial, state or other political subdivision taxes which may be more burdensome than the applicable national taxes. One must be certain to determine the applicable amounts of taxes which may be charged to an estate in every country in which the deceased held real or personal property. Also know and understand the state inheritance tax laws which may affect your estate. Substantial additional amounts may be payable because of differing inheritance tax laws of the various states. And last, there are major income and capital gain tax considerations which must be allowed for.

For estates of decedents who died after 1980, the credit under applicable Federal law provides a tax-free transfer of the estate whether by gift during lifetime and/or at death. (Amounts are shown in Chart 9.1.) The amount of credit *in and after* 1987 will be $600,000 per individual. This means a husband and wife, beginning in 1987, may transfer as much as $1,200,000 (two times $600,000) with proper planning and without incurring gift or estate taxes under the unified transfer tax program.

You should be aware, however, that the unified transfer taxes increase at an accelerated rate after the exempt amount is excluded and goes from rates of 34% to 37% to the maximum tax under current law of 55% on each estate.

In determining your estate planning fundamentals you must define the composition of the estate, that is, what you own and what is owed and the present value of your assets. The at-law estate liabilities which must be paid at your death or thereafter are included. Secondly, consider the goals and objectives for yourself and your family. Communication between husband and wife should take place on a continuing basis if the estate plan is to be meaningful. Planning goals and objectives for both husband and wife while alive, and for one when the death of the other occurs, and for the family in the event that both parents die means, of course, the formulation of a death strategy.

A death strategy involves an understanding of the following: First, identify the probate county or surrogate court that will have jurisdiction over the estate. Second, minimize, through all available legal and financial activities, additional probate proceedings. The probate proceeding in the state in which you live at the time of your death is known as the domiciliary probate proceeding. All real estate and mineral interests will be transferred according to the laws of the state in which the property is located. Personal property, stocks, bonds, CD's or personal effects will be transferred according to the laws of the state in which you live. Additional or ancillary probate proceedings can often be avoided by the transfer of title to real estate and mineral interest to various trusts and/or corporations. Next, undertake to reduce estate transfer costs by simplifying the probate procedure. We will discuss this more fully in Chapter 10, but you should be aware that there are many ways today whereby one may reduce the estate transfer costs. Prearranged plans for the disposition of an estate can avoid many headaches associated with probate procedure and avoid unnecessary transfer fees and professional costs.

Next, be certain you provide sufficient liquidity to meet liabilities and taxes which will become due and payable at your death. And finally, coordinate your corporate, private and public benefit programs, and incentive compensation beneficiary designations along with your insurance designations in formulating an overall death strategy.

Then, of course, create a will-trust system that executes your strategy. Be certain you use a qualified estate planning attorney. The American Bar Association now has such a specialized designation in the practice of law. Seek recommendations for a reputable professional estate planning specialist when searching for a qualified attorney to prepare your will and/or trust instruments. The specialists should assist with your overall estate planning.

Next, identify the disposition of personal effects. Avoid allowing members of the family to get into unnecessary quarrels and to develop emotional attitudes which can result in displacement and unhappiness within the family unit. I have witnessed, too often, family members disagreeing over such minor items as who should get eggs the chickens laid. Devote adequate attention to the minor along with the major, important matters needing cooperation and support in the overall administration of the estate. Otherwise too many family members may inadvertently find themselves "majoring in minors" at an inopportune time.

Next, use trusts where appropriate. We will discuss trusts more thoroughly in Chapter 10. Be certain you select an executor and a trustee qualified to settle your estate and administer the various trusts you decide to create. I will talk about qualifications for an executor and a trustee later in this chapter.

Decide who the beneficiaries of your estate are to be and determine in this connection two more important matters. First, are you going to leave your property or bequest outright or in trusts for the beneficiary designated? If the beneficiary is a minor or a person with inexperience in business matters or in poor health or aging you might want to consider the use of a trust through which the properties would pass with professional management, as opposed to outright bequests for others. Secondly, you should determine either the *dollar amount* or *percentage* of your net estate you wish each beneficiary to have. I recommend you use a dollar amount for specific bequests to charities or individuals. Leave the residue estate, after the specific bequests have been satisfied and applicable taxes paid and debts satisfied, as a percentage or a fraction of the estate to the remaining beneficiaries, respectively. This may prevent your inadvertently providing for more or less than intended to each of the various beneficiaries.

Prepare a personal net worth statement showing what your assets and liabilities are anticipated to amount to at death. An after-death balance sheet is substantially different from a living balance sheet for the following reasons: (1) Your company benefits will normally vest 100% at your death. (2) Your life insurance should be shown on your statement as the face value of the life insurance instead of the cash value while you are living. You should also show the estimated estate or transfer tax as well as state inheritance taxes due at your death as a *liability* in your post-death net worth statement. From the net worth calculated under this formula you will be able to get a reasonably accurate estimate of the total liabilities and taxes. For purposes of determining the next important step in your financial strategy, prepare your estate composition at death in terms of a liquid assets schedule. Chart 9.2 illustrates a typical estate in terms of liquid assets, immediate debts and other assets. There is no federal estate or transfer tax due because, in this case, John Doe left everything to his wife under the unlimited marital deduction. The amount of the estate that is liquid in terms of the mere $86,264 in debts will be more than adequate to satisfy the immediate debts and taxes due. If, however, there is no marital survivor, the liquidity requirement will be substantially different. Important point: Include the vested amount of your benefit plans and the face value of your life insurance in determining the liquid portion of your estate along with marketable securities and cash. Be certain you make as accurate an estimate as is possible of debts and taxes against which you compare your liquid assets. Make certain your plan will prevent your fixed assets being sold to satisfy debts or taxes. When assets are hurriedly sold to meet tax requirements, history indicates the average estate is lucky to get 50¢ on the dollar.

As an integral part of your estate planning strategy always undertake to arrive at a realistic net estate value to be distributed to your heirs *after* both husband and wife are deceased. From your gross estate you should deduct those amounts of debts and taxes that must be paid, as shown on Chart 9.3, along with other liabilities. Include any transfer tax liability accruing from the first to die, then the adjusted amount goes to the estate of the survivor (second to die) and will further be reduced by federal transfer taxes and state transfer taxes or foreign transfer taxes, together with any additional debts. From that will come the net estate figure which will be the amount distributed to your intended heirs. The point to remember is the *net estate* is always substantially different from the gross estate and should be carefully calculated in

143

Defining Estate Composition (At Death)

John Doe

Liquid Asset Schedule

Liquid Assets		
Cash	$ 8,000	
Marketable Stock	12,000	
Notes Receivable	10,000	
Savings Plan	300,000	
Stock Option Bargain Element	90,000	
Retirement Benefit	60,000	
Life Insurance Proceeds	800,000	
Social Security Death Benefit	255	1,280,255
Immediate Debts		
Death Expenses	$ 33,864	
Federal Estate Tax	0	
Notes Payable	3,000	
Taxes Due	45,900	
Insurance Loans	3,500	(86,264)
Net Liquid Assets		1,193,991
Other Assets (Net)		
Automobiles	$ 9,000	
Home	90,000	
Vacation Home	35,000	
Personal Property	75,000	
Household Furnishings	35,000	$ 244,000
Total Net Assets		$ 1,437,991

Assuming You Have Your Wills Updated to Comply With ERTA of 1981

CHART 9.2

Calculation Of Net Estate

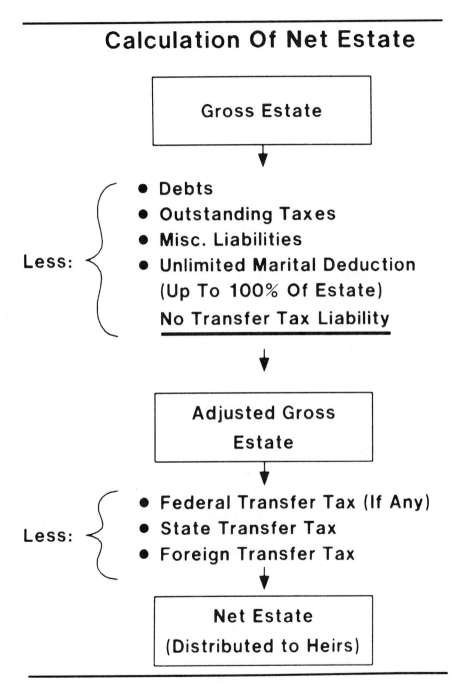

```
                  ┌─────────────────────┐
                  │    Gross Estate     │
                  └─────────────────────┘
                             ↓
```

• Debts
• Outstanding Taxes
• Misc. Liabilities
• Unlimited Marital Deduction
(Up To 100% Of Estate)

Less: { ... }

No Transfer Tax Liability

```
                  ┌─────────────────────┐
                  │   Adjusted Gross    │
                  │       Estate        │
                  └─────────────────────┘
                             ↓
```

• Federal Transfer Tax (If Any)
• State Transfer Tax
• Foreign Transfer Tax

Less: { ... }

```
                  ┌─────────────────────┐
                  │     Net Estate      │
                  │(Distributed to Heirs)│
                  └─────────────────────┘
```

CHART 9.3

order for you and your spouse to adequately determine what each intended recipient will actually receive in approximate dollar amounts. Naturally, this form of sophisticated "bottom line" planning calls for annual reviewing if it is to remain meaningful and accurate.

Human Factors in Estate Planning

There is not a more important part of your overall estate planning strategy than consideration of the *human factors*. (Chart 9.4) We have dealt with the legal procedures involved in preparing a last will and testament and the probate procedures, along with the estate settlement. We have examined the responsibilities of the executor in the settlement of a typical estate—all of which are important elements in your estate planning strategy.

But the human factor is the most misunderstood and most often neglected of all the key components of any estate planning strategy. You must remember that estate planning is really a matter of education, a learning experience for you and your spouse as well as for all the members of your family, more important than all the university degrees in the world. Today, there are three adult generations living and in reasonably good health in most typical family units. My experience indicates that sadly enough they are not communicating with each other relative to their intentions for the disposition of their respective estates. Uncle Sam, believe it or not, is the chief beneficiary of this failure to communicate. He'll likely collect a great deal more from the estates of the non-communicators than from those estates which have been prudently planned. Much can be accomplished if ample time is spent with each other simply undertaking to understand the other's needs and desires and to coordinate the estate planning of the various generations. Maximum benefits accrue to the family when there is valid understanding and dialog between generations.

Please keep in mind that we are dealing with fundamental human emotions when we develop estate planning strategies: uncertainty, insecurity and three great motivating factors—*fear* of loss, *hope* for gain and the *need* for love and affection. No one wants to lose when planning an estate. We are always *hopeful* for more. We are doing something which should express an act of sincere love and affection. My unhappy experience, however, is that many times, unknowingly and unintentionally, we do things *to* people rather than *for* them when dispersing our properties. Estate planning is an act affecting your lifetime as well as future generations. Sometimes we can cause severe family displacement, career deviation problems and unnecessary guilt feelings by the way we handle or mishandle the disposition of properties.

To avoid this, it seems to me, the prudent person should seek to gain a clear knowledge of *family characteristics*. What are the ages? What are you considering giving and how many people are involved? You can think of a dozen more questions that must be asked—and answered responsibly. It is

Human Factors In Estate Planning

- **Estate Planning Is a Matter of Education**
- **Deal With Fundamental Human Emotions**
    - **Uncertainty/Insecurity**
    - **Fear of Loss**
    - **Hope for Gain**
    - **Love/Affection**
- **Family Planning**
    - **During Your Lifetime**
    - **For Next Generation**
- **Have a Clear Knowledge of**
    - **Family Characteristics**
    - **Family Goals/Objectives**
    - **Family Assets/Liabilities**
    - **Family Tax Position**

CHART 9.4

clearly a difficult consideration to leave money or property to minor children rather than to mature adults. If property is left to a minor child, a guardian will have to be appointed to manage the properties until the child reaches maturity. Normally the guardianship will terminate at 21 years of age which, in my judgment, is too early for young people to assume the management of sufficient amounts of property. You may want to use a trust for the younger people and/or other members of the family who may be precluded from managing their property due to health problems, age, lack of experience or other factors.

By the same token you must consider the significant problems which are as certain as death itself when leaving an estate of a million dollars to ten people as opposed to one. The amount each recipient will receive obviously will vary and could alter choices of how one will provide for each legacy. What is the marital status of members of your family and what are the potential inheritances from the other side of the marital relationship? If your son, Johnny, has married a lady whose parents have significant resources and are already making gifts to your grandchildren, you might want to consider an alternate course for the disposition of your estate than you would otherwise contemplate. This course of action may avoid further complicating an already involved estate planning situation. What is the education of each prospective beneficiary? What is the vocational interest of each? What are their individual business experiences?

More important than all of these, perhaps, is what are their interest and ability to manage property or investments? How much are you calling on them to do that which may be counterproductive to them as far as their career pursuits are concerned? My experience shows that most people are not interested in becoming married to a family inheritance; on the other hand, they feel guilty if they neglect it. One must take these facts and factors into account when thinking about what one will do for various family members. Outright bequests or the use of a trust device may be a possible answer. Other methods are available—depending on your answers to these many questions.

In considering additional family characteristics you should think about their individual spending habits. Do you have a spendthrift family member? Are your prospective beneficiaries conservative? And what is their mental and physical health and their emotional state? One can easily accentuate health problems through the unwise disposition of assets.

What are the objectives of the various members of the family? Are you about to do something that will supplement or complement their goals, or will you cause severe deviation from those objectives? Be sensitive to the individual needs of the various members of the family: their feelings, their attitudes, their goals, their objectives, their personalities; theirs are not the same as yours in most instances. To do an effective and meaningful job of disposing of an estate, you should undertake to complement the lifestyle of your loved ones and intended beneficiaries as opposed to enforcing a form of financial discipline upon them, even though unintended, through the manner in which the estate is ultimately distributed.

Next, *consider your assets and your liabilities.* Examine your assets in terms of why you acquired them and why you continue to hold them, and ask yourself whether they satisfy the purposes for which they were acquired in the first place. Examine whether these assets are meeting your needs at the present time. In addition, think in terms of whether the assets will be suitable for your family after your death. You cannot legally take property out of commerce by providing that it never be sold under your will or trust arrangements. You can often have a strong negative emotional impact on others by implying or instructing your descendants to never sell a given piece of property or stock. I have seen this conduct result in disastrous financial difficulties later because a deceased mother once said *never sell the farm,* and the property today is clearly not worth retaining. The fact is the farm is now a serious economic drain on the family's wealth, but no one wants to accept the responsibility of liquidating it. What was good for you as an investment may not be a desirable property for your family or your spouse after you depart this world. Secondly, under current tax laws all of the assets of a deceased get a "stepped-up basis" as of the date of death of either spouse. This simply means that tax considerations for holding appreciated assets are no longer valid. The family now has greater flexibility in changing or altering investments, without possible unfavorable tax considerations which may have existed before the death.

Other considerations for examination of assets should include the ability of the property to produce income, cost of maintenance, and the family's possible emotional involvement with the asset. We clearly are better buyers than sellers. We have a natural weakness to become emotionally involved with assets and tend to pass them on to others without considering the consequences. Care should be taken here. Be as objective as possible in evaluating family assets and leave maximum flexibility to the executor and/or trustee to change or alter the assets based on prevailing socio-economic-political situations. Flexibility should be provided to meet all of the family's needs through the years of the administration of the estate and the resultant trust.

Clearly examine all of your liabilities. Why did you borrow the money? From whom did you borrow the money? How is the money to be repaid? Is payment clearly to the advantage of the estate and the family at your death? Wills often provide for the payment of all debts and liabilities when the mortgages involved on certain types of real estate, including the home, may be very difficult to replace. It may be advantageous to the family *not* to pay some indebtedness. It is certainly different to owe a family member a significant amount of money than it is to owe it to a bank. Employees of major corporations should realize that sometimes a lending institution was more friendly to them while they were connected with their employer than they might be to the family after the death of the employee. There are many reasons for carefully examining your liabilities and being realistic about determinations of the debt after your death.

149

Most people assume they should provide in their wills that debts are to be paid before the assets are distributed. It's standard boilerplate in many of the "do-it-yourself" will-writing guides. Even many so-called competent attorneys mistakenly—and perhaps innocently—*think* they are giving sound advice when they dispense this pay-the-debt recommendation to their clients. However, it is not always in the best interest of the estate or the descendants.

We recently were involved in a medium-size estate where a substantial amount of the inheritance was in the form of a large home and farm. Both properties were mortgaged at interest rates well below the market. Instead of using the limited cash in the estate to retire the debt, the funds were made available for investment. The positive difference between the yield from the investments and the interest payable on the two mortgages came to approximately five percentage points. Had the will called for the repayment of debts, this estate would have had serious cash-flow problems, and the executor would most likely have been *forced* to sell the home, the farm or both. Instead, the estate was kept intact and enjoyed a favorable cash flow while the descendants enjoyed the use of the real estate.

Last, but certainly not least, think in terms of the family's tax position. Notice here that we've again been talking about personal-financial-economic considerations before considering the tax position. Too often too much estate planning strategy involves simple transfer tax, income or capital gain tax reduction methods and in the process causes severe displacement and other difficulties in terms of the human factors involved. If we can accomplish our objectives—including family considerations, goals and objectives—and at the same time maintain our asset and liability posture and reduce our transfer tax and/or income taxes, then by all means we should. If, however, tax deduction methods are in conflict with family requirements, characteristics, goals and objectives, obviously we should defer to the family needs ahead of tax considerations.

Fiduciary Terms

There are several specific fiduciary terms with which everyone should be familiar. The *trust* is a legal arrangement created by an individual directing the duties of a trustee and the rights of beneficiaries relative to the assets held in trust. The trust therefore is a legal person, the same as is a corporation or a real live person. Legal title is transferred to a trust upon its creation. Beneficial ownership vests in the beneficiaries of the trust. There are three parties to most trust arrangements. The *trustee* is the fiduciary, somebody who is responsible for administering the trust as governed by the trust document. This normally is a competent adult person or a bank or trust company qualified to serve in a fiduciary capacity. Fiduciary capacity means the capacity or responsibility to honorably manage the properties in trust and for the intended purposes and for the benefit of the beneficiary. The *grantor* of the trust is the one who establishes the trust. The corpus of the trust is another term for the assets in trust. The *beneficiary* is the recipient of income or principal or both from the trust.

There are many valid reasons for creating a trust. Among them are (1) to place the burden of property and investment management in the hands of an experienced trustee; (2) to allow the trustee to use his discretion in handling the trust property for the benefit of the beneficiaries; (3) to protect the grantor's and his or her descendants against demands and entreaties made by well meaning, or not so well meaning, third parties; (4) to provide property management for minors, mentally retarded and others, and the avoidance of guardianships; (5) to protect the beneficiaries from themselves in the event of problems involving physical, mental, emotional or spendthrift attitudes and habits; (6) the management of a business interest after death; and (7) to provide flexibility for dealing with income, capital gain and estate tax planning problems.

The trust in its original form was a derivative of Roman law and which ultimately came to us through English law. Trusts evolved from what was originally termed "simple trust" to the more complex trusts of today. Under early trusts property was placed in escrow with no provision for the change of investments, and all income from the corpus was distributed to specified beneficiaries with the remainder going to the ultimate beneficiaries at a specific date or occurrence as dictated in the trust documents. As our society progressed through the years it was determined that it was not always wise to retain the original assets placed into a trust. When trusts initially became popular in the United States grantors tended to provide for the disposition of assets in trusts and, in many instances, required the purchase of government bonds as an alternate investment. Later several of the states provided for "legal lists" of investments, that is, investments which were approved by the respective state legislatures as suitable for investments by trustees. This matter, of course, soon became a political football and subsequent legislation provided for what we now know as the *prudent man rule* for investments. Under most current trust arrangements the trustee has the authority to change investments in the management of property into investments that a "prudent man" would normally be expected to invest in for his own account. Prudent-man rules tend to discourage speculation.

Later it was determined that occasionally the income from the trust may not be sufficient under certain circumstances to meet educational, health or emergency requirements of a given beneficiary. Therefore, the laws were amended and provide discretion on the part of the trustee. Under modern instruments a trustee may be allowed to invade the corpus or the principal of the trust for purposes of satisfying needs of the beneficiaries. With a *spray provision,* as it has come to be called in trust agreements, the trustee may elect to distribute a portion of the income to a widow and her three children for example, retaining remaining income in the trust. In this situation there are five taxpayers: the wife, three children and the trust. Income otherwise could be required to be distributed to the wife with applicable income taxes being much higher on one recipient than if the distribution is divided into five entities.

Most trust instruments provide discretion to the trustee in determining how much income to distribute and to which beneficiaries. If Johnny, as mentioned earlier, had married a young lady whose family had already provided substantial assets for her and Johnny during their lifetimes or in testamentary transfers, then Johnny's trust need not terminate into Johnny's estate bringing with it additional tax burden. The trustees may have discretion to hold the trust for Johnny's children. In many instances today trusts have provisions allowing the trustee discretion in determining whether or not a trust should terminate or remain in effect for the benefit of the beneficiary and with a portion of the corpus passing on to the beneficiary's descendants. This method of distribution will avoid possible transfer tax in the original beneficiary's estate. The point is that the discretion afforded the trustee under the modern trusts allows for a great deal of flexibility in the handling of a trust's assets and in the disposition of both income and principal assets. Of course the trustee is usually bonded and may be held accountable and liable for his actions.

I call your attention to the importance of these varied provisions and options when considering the selection of a trustee. The grantor is, in effect, asking the trustee to make Solomon-like decisions. Most people are called upon from time to time to make crucial choices for various members of the family. This may involve complicated and emotional decisions, e.g., decisions that involve distributions to provide for the payment of support payments for a father who is not supporting his children and using the assets of the children's trust to provide for the father's lifestyle. A request for money under the discretionary provision for an abortion for a 14-year old beneficiary is an example of the difficult decisions and choices a trustee may be called upon to make. Expecting a trustee to make these kinds of decisions in our absence is overwhelming to say the least. Yet that's the role of the trustee. I have had to face all of these types of decisions and many more in my career as a trust officer. They involve human factors which are extremely difficult to deal with—decisions that are next to impossible to decide in terms of fairness and certainty about what is best for all parties involved.

The selection of a trustee is obviously extremely important. Equally as important is the selection of an executor. How much time do most spend in considering whom to ask to carry out these most important duties and responsibilities? I feel that an individual should invest a great deal of time and careful thought in this matter. Be certain those whom you are considering to serve as your executor or trustee are aware that you have named them in those capacities and that you have obtained their willingness to serve. You are not doing a favor or bestowing a great honor when naming a person your executor or trustee. You are asking him to devote a substantial amount of time and energy to manage the affairs of the estate. The person named must manage, with a considerable amount of discretion, the investments of the trust and be responsible for all distribution powers under the will and trust instruments. You also are subjecting his personal estates to substantial potential liabilities. Should he fail to adequately execute the responsibilities which you have given, either through errors of omission or errors of commission, the trustee can be held personally liable.

In the matter of the selection of trustees for minor children be certain those you propose to name as trustees are aware of these most important appointments and have indicated a willingness to serve. Too often I have been faced with situations where both parents have been killed and their minor children designated to specific in-laws as guardians of the estate, and the in-laws knew nothing about the appointments. In many instances, the in-laws have been unable to serve in these capacities due to marital difficulties or financial restrictions preventing them from accepting the responsibilities. You can probably imagine the ensuing problems and the potential damage to the psyches of frightened and confused orphans.

My general suggestion is to consider selecting a professional executor or trustee such as a bank or trust company. Visit the bank or trust company, get acquainted with its staff, understand its policies and procedures. If possible do business with them through the years so you can get a feeling of the culture of that organization and make certain it fits your requirements and expectations. Consider your family's needs and objectives when evaluating and selecting a professional executor and trustee.

One last thought. After many years of consideration it seems to me that a co-executorship relationship of a professional fiduciary, such as a bank or trust company, and an individual family member provides the best answer to the challenge for naming an executor and trustee. By naming co-executors and co-trustees you have the best of all worlds. The personal relationship of the family member and the professional's expertise and competence should provide a satisfactory relationship in meeting the obligations of the executor and trustee.

In considering the qualifications of an executor and trustee search out individuals with the following traits and skills: (1) responsibility and maturity; (2) balanced objectivity and Solomon-like understanding; (3) financial responsibility and perpetuity (the average trust lasts twenty years); (4) avoidance of conflicts of interest between the estate and its beneficiaries and the executor's or trustee's personal and business interests; (5) experience in managing investments and property; and (6) a full understanding of all the applicable legal and tax laws involved.

I strongly recommend that the instruments (will and trusts) include provisions allowing the executor and trustee to resign with or without cause. By the same token I feel a member of the family should have the right to change the corporate trustee should the relationship prove undesirable or unmanageable. In some cases this right could be extended to a group of family members such as a simple majority where two or more agree to seek a change.

As you will better understand after reading Chapter 10, I am addressing all activities within the entire financial life cycle when detailing the subject of estate planning, starting from the simple format of considerations in the formation period to the more complex decisions involving the family and, as the family grows and matures and asset accumulations become larger and more diverse, the needs of the changing unit. You will find by spending the necessary time to think through the many-fold considerations involved in estate planning strategy, your decisions relative to disposing of property will force intelligent decisions. This is especially true while accumulating property and as you progress through the complete financial life cycle. Caution: do not neglect any aspect nor overlook any steps mentioned. All are important in terms of providing peace of mind and knowing you have been constructive in both the accumulations as well as the disposition. (Chart 9.5)

CASE HISTORY I

A lady who came in not too long ago had just found her husband's will three days after his death only to learn that the document had not been updated. He had left *everything* to his ex-wife. This happened in a community property state so she would at least receive one-half of any community property accumulation during their two-year marriage. Unfortunately for the widow, it was a very nominal sum indeed. It was clear from other evidence that her husband had no intention of leaving his estate to his ex-wife. To the contrary. But through simple neglect and by failing to keep his will up-to-date, it turned out he did everything for an ex-wife and nothing for his new spouse.

CASE HISTORY II

Several years ago I managed a trust for the benefit of two children whose parents had died within six months of one another. The deaths had occurred many years earlier. The children had lived in an orphanage. Provision had been made through a trust for the children's incidental expenses to be paid to the orphanage providing for basic lifestyle costs. Social Security was collected for both children during their minority. By the time I assumed responsibility for the trust the girl was ready to enter college. The children had since come to live with an uncle. The little boy did very well in his schooling.

The daughter, however, had difficulty in maturing and had incurred substantial psychological therapy expenses. She had difficulty in entering into a university and then flunked out. As trustee I helped get her a job and assisted in getting her back into a university of her choice. She promptly failed again and lost the job. This pattern continued for two years. During that time I noticed the daughter's department store bills included such luxury items as

Avoid Perils Of Procrastination

● **Dying Intestate (Without a Will)**

  —Disposition to Heirs at Improper Time/Improper Amounts

  —Court Appointed Administrator

  —Loss of Possible Estate Tax Advantages

  —State Descent and Distribution Laws Apply (State Prepare Will)

● **Dying With an Obsolete Will**

  —Inappropriate Executor

  —Failure to Include Intended Beneficiary

  —Loss of Estate and Income Tax Opportunities

  —Failure to Consider Changes in Composition and Size of Estate

● **Illiquid Estate**

  —Forced Liquidation of Fixed Assets

CHART 9.5

155

pedicures and manicures. We promptly rearranged our methods for the payment of her bills. We paid the university direct for tuition and books. We curtailed the opportunities for extravagant spending of her allowance.

Later she again quit her job, dropped out of school and purchased a new car. She told me that she wanted to get married. Her husband-to-be was from a mideastern country. She asked for distributions from the trust for a washer and dryer, refrigerator/freezer and to pay off a note on the automobile. After consultation with her minister, psychiatrist and her uncle, we determined not to make the distributions at that time but instead advised her we would make arrangements for these items after she was settled in her new home. (She planned to live in the groom's native country.)

Several weeks later she told me I was right in not making the distribution and that the young man was not right for her. They were not going to get married and she planned to return to the university. Two weeks later she returned to tell me she was pregnant and married, in that order, and that her husband's visa was up and they were leaving for his homeland. Within two weeks we made distributions for maternity clothes and made arrangements for her travel expenses. Over the next few years I seldom heard from her. I felt our determination not to distribute more funds would possibly discourage a permanent move to the Middle East. This was occasioned by the fact that her newborn child was a citizen of the father's country. I was advised by the minister and psychiatrist if she returned to the States, she might not be able to bring the child.

I made arrangements through a foreign bank for money for an airline ticket to the United States should she desire to return. Several years later she used the letter of credit to obtain an airline ticket. She came back badly beaten, seeking a divorce and feeling totally distraught about having to leave her child with the father. I arranged for additional consultation and sought and found her a new job, and later her husband and child were reunited with her. To my knowledge they are still married and enjoying a very happy and productive career and family life.

I shall never forget the key decisions which had to be made under stressful circumstances. This is a dramatic, yet very real, illustration of the discretion which trustees normally must exercise in carrying out or executing the wishes of a grantor under trust arrangements.

CASE HISTORY III

Several years earlier, in another state, a family group called on a bank which was trustee of their father's estate. As trustee the bank held a portfolio of stocks purchased by the deceased father. They asked that the bank sell all the common stock and purchase bonds. Following careful research the family group believed the stockmarket was too high and that bonds were safer investments.

The bank refused, but upon presentation of letters of indemnity signed by all family members, the bank acquiesced, sold the stock and bought bonds. As it turned out the value of the stock enhanced substantially. Several years later one of the grandchildren who had since grown to maturity came into the bank with her lawyer demanding that she be paid the difference between what her parents' share of the estate would have been had the stock *not* been sold, plus interest on the difference for all the years since the time of the sale of the stocks.

The court awarded the young lady a substantial judgement, emphasizing that the bank's obligation was to serve and carry out the wishes of the testator (the creator of the trust) and not to bend to the wishes of the beneficiaries. The court said that if the creator of the trust wanted the beneficiaries to make investment decisions the grantor would have left the property to them in the first place. The responsibility, said the court, of the executor and trustee is to the creator of the trust or the testator of the will and *not* to the beneficiaries.

These facts should be kept in mind when determining what you want to do with your estate and even more importantly, when selecting an executor and trustee. The executor's and trustee's duties are to carry out *your* wishes, not those of the family.

Chapter Ten

THE "STEREO COMPONENT" SCENARIO

Now that I have detailed the Personal Financial Life Cycle and we have examined the components for adequate personal financial planning, it is time, as the modern-day saying goes, to "get it together."

Thus, the purpose of this final chapter.

I take the approach of a modular or "component" organization. That is, a system that builds financial planning in steps—or components—as the individual's or the family's circumstances change and as various financial needs dictate. There are two fundamental reasons for this approach. First, every person's and every family's resources and requirements are distinctly different. It is necessary that each be able to "tailor" financial planning accordingly. The individual and the family must have options—rather than be faced with the almost impossible task of putting together a single comprehensive financial plan covering *all* needs for the rest of their lives. Second, the component approach provides maximum flexibility for sound financial planning, and in this rapidly changing financial world, flexibility is an absolute must, a necessity—not merely a luxury.

I compare this approach to the development of an increasingly sophisticated stereo sound system. The individual or the family begins with an empty room and initially adds a few basic components—simple, single-purpose financial instruments or trusts, for example, that may be compared to a basic stereo receiver with two simple speakers. As the family's resources increase and its tastes grow more discriminating and sophisticated, other components are added . . . or earlier ones are modified or even replaced. Soon the room is filled with woofers, tweeters, turntables, digital systems, amplifiers, flashing lights, tape decks—the whole nine yards.

Thus, our "financial stereo system" is continually refined and expanded as the individual and the family move through the Personal Financial Life Cycle, from the initial Formation Period all the way through the Preservation Period of their later lives.

THE DOE FAMILY: TWO ASSUMPTIONS

Let's travel with John and Mary Doe, a typical family, through their Personal Financial Life Cycle and see whether we can determine some of the programs—or "components"—they should consider. First, two assumptions . . .

1. John and Mary make rather interesting financial progress as they move along. We cannot, of course, assume this for everyone. It has been my experience that people generally achieve a higher standard of living with stable income when they do not need repeat buying of many of the durable "big ticket" items that are usually purchased early on. I refer to such assets as a home, household furnishings and automobiles. Funds that would be used to re-purchase those items can be devoted to other purposes— lifestyle enhancement and/or savings for the production of additional income.

2. John and Mary have taken care of the financial essentials discussed in previous chapters. They have adequate insurance; they have used credit wisely and not abused it; they have maintained sound levels of liquidity; they have put in place adequate depreciation programs for replacement purposes and have monitored and controlled their cash flow as they progress through the life cycle.

THE FORMATION PERIOD

With these two assumptions in mind, we can now set a course upon which a typical family who is accumulating assets and progressing financially may embark on an estate-planning program. Initially, we start with the Formation Period in which John and Mary Doe financially look like this (Chart 10.1 and 10.2):

The importance of wills has been covered in the preceding chapter. I will illustrate and underscore the necessity of an up-to-date will by showing how it "fits" with the Revocable Living Trust.

The Revocable Living Trust: Our Basic Stereo Component

The basic financial stereo system calls for the development of a Revocable Living Trust or, as I label it the Family Trust. (Chart 10.3) This is a highly flexible financial planning vehicle, call it "Hi-Fi," with many important and desirable features. Examples are:

- The Trust can be an investment vehicle while both John and Mary are living.
- The Trust can act on their behalf if one or both of them become incapacitated.
- Assets contributed to the Trust are not subject to probate and, therefore, are not items of public record. This helps ensure privacy for the family and minimizes probate costs and professional fees.
- When John or Mary die the trustee may be authorized to buy assets from or lend money to John's or Mary's estate. This enables the estate's executor to transfer liquid assets to the estate for the payment of debts and taxes.
- Certain company benefits may be made payable to the Trust.
- Insurance policy beneficiary designations may be made payable to the Trust, thereby avoiding multifold wills.
- Keogh plans, IRA rollovers and IRA's may be made payable to the Trust.

Under this plan John's and Mary's wills may be rather simple. They need only name their executors, leaving their personal effects and making specific bequests to whomever they please, and then designate the residue of their estate payable to the Revocable Living or Family Trust. (Chart 10.4)

A desirable feature of this type of trust, as its name implies, is that it is revocable. This trust can be changed as frequently as John and Mary wish and may even be terminated at their discretion.

One final feature of the Revocable Living Trust: John's and Mary's wills need only be changed when the family moves from one state to another to conform to the state laws in which they are then residing. The Trust need not be changed or redrawn with each move, nor must the distributions specified in the wills be altered.

Kanaly Trust Company

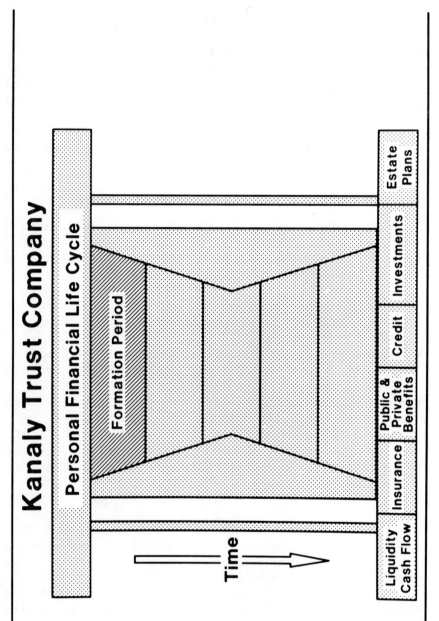

Personal Financial Life Cycle

Formation Period

Time

Liquidity Cash Flow | Insurance | Public & Private Benefits | Credit | Investments | Estate Plans

CHART 10.1

Formation Period

Personal Financial Life Cycle

Age
25–35 Years Old

Income
$35,000–$60,000/Year

Net Worth
$70,000

Life Insurance
$300,000–$400,000

Estate Size
$370,000–$400,000

Estate Systems to Consider

- Will, Husband and Wife
- Revocable Living Trust
- Bypass Trust

CHART 10.2

Revocable Living Trust

- Investment Vehicle While Living

- Act in Your Behalf if You Become Incapacitated

- Contributed Assets Not Subject to Probate and Therefore Not an Item of Public Record

- Probate Costs and Attorney's Fees are Minimized

CHART 10.3

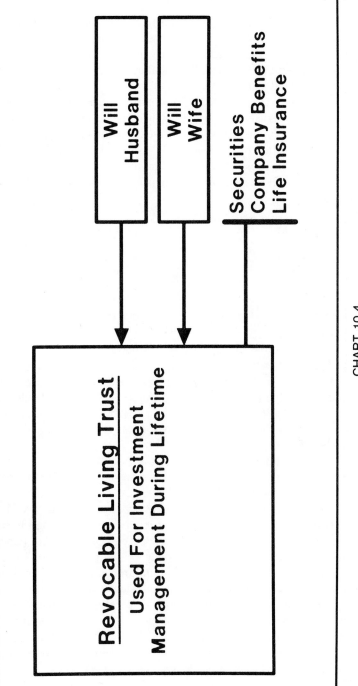

Will
Husband

Will
Wife

Securities
Company Benefits
Life Insurance

Revocable Living Trust

Used For Investment
Management During Lifetime

CHART 10.4

The Bypass Trust—Our Next Component

Because of the $300,000 to $400,000 worth of life insurance we have assumed for John and Mary Doe they should consider a Bypass Trust. (Chart 10.5) Even at this relatively early stage of their lives and in this first phase of Personal Financial Life Cycle, the Bypass makes a lot of sense. The Bypass Trust is our next financial stereo component.

The Bypass Trust is funded by the distributive portions of the Revocable Living or Family Trust with that amount of money which qualifies for the Transfer Tax Exemption Equivalent. Present tax laws allow for increases to a maximum of $600,000 by the year 1987. It is sometimes known as a Unified Credit. In the case of estates of those who died in 1983 or later the Unified Credit provides an escalating tax-free transfer of amounts from the decedent's estate as shown:

Year	Tax-Free Transfer
1981	$175,000
1982	225,000
1983	275,000
1984	325,000
1985	400,000
1986	500,000
1987 and thereafter	600,000

This Bypass Trust will be for the benefit of the survivor or survivors of John and Mary Doe and the survivors' children. The trust should be established to last at least the lifetime of the surviving spouse, with income and principal to be distributed to the survivor or survivors or the children at the trustee's discretion.

Any appreciation in the trust assets will be transferred tax free to the children or to other beneficiaries. Proceeds are not taxed in this trust when John or Mary dies or when the surviving spouse dies.

Clearly, there are substantial income tax advantages involved in the use of this trust. The income from the trust can be spread among the survivors' children and other beneficiaries, including parents, if so desired. (Chart 10.6)

As John and Mary Doe move along through their Formation Period, they will likely acquire offspring and, as children are apt to bring with them, a somewhat broader perspective. John and Mary's children are now rapidly growing up. John and Mary have, through careful planning, taken care of their primary household formation expenses. Now the Does are adjusting themselves to their futures.

In short, they are ready to move—or be moved by their circumstances and needs—into the Orientation Period. (Chart 10.7)

Bypass Trust

- Funded With Exemption Equivalent (Transfer Tax-Free)

- For the Benefit of Survivor and Children

- Asset Appreciation is Transferred Tax-Free to Children or Other Beneficiaries

CHART 10.5

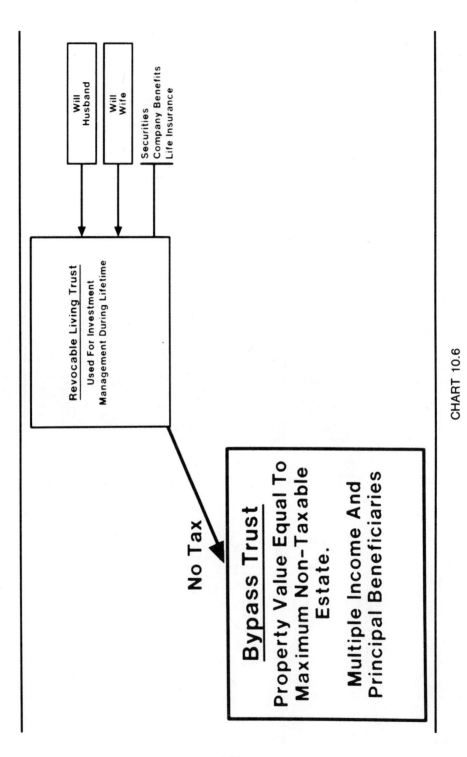

Will
Husband

Will
Wife

Securities
Company Benefits
Life Insurance

Revocable Living Trust

Used For Investment
Management During Lifetime

No Tax

Bypass Trust

Property Value Equal To
Maximum Non-Taxable
Estate.

Multiple Income And
Principal Beneficiaries

CHART 10.6

Kanaly Trust Company

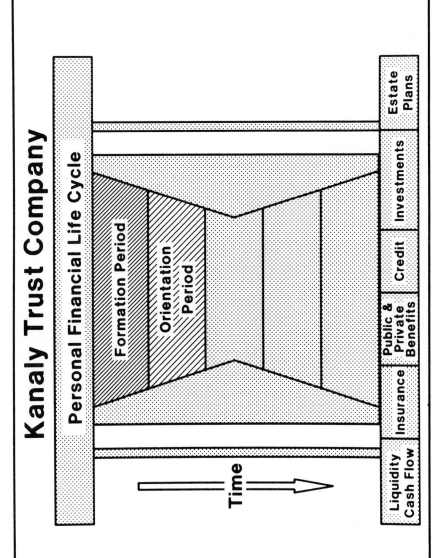

CHART 10.7

THE ORIENTATION PERIOD

As John and Mary Doe enter this second phase of their Personal Financial Life Cycle, financially they are starting to look something like this (Chart 10.8):

The Marital Trust

We will assume the Family and Bypass Trusts remain in place and examine the new Marital Trust. (Chart 10.9 and 10.10)

The principal purpose of the Marital Trust is to provide a trust for the convenience of the surviving spouse following the death of John or Mary.

The Marital Trust includes only the survivor's property, i.e., the property left to him or her by the deceased spouse. Property which was jointly held or owned under the state's community property laws and that property which was received prior to or during the marriage from the survivor's family are included.

The surviving spouse has total control over these assets. That is, John or Mary can terminate the trust and give the assets to whom he or she pleases or pass them by testamentary disposition or by will, as he or she desires.

The Qualified Terminal Interest Trust, or "Q-TIP"

John and Mary's joint estate is now large enough to call for consideration of the Qualified Terminal Interest Trust, or Q-TIP as it is commonly known. (Chart 10.11. and 10.12) This trust is funded with any portion of the unlimited marital deduction property. One-hundred percent of the income must go to the survivor during his or her lifetime; however, the disposition of the property in trust at the death of the survivor will be handled according to the testamentary provisions of the first deceased's desires.

John and Mary Doe are still relatively young. Should one of them die at an early age, the survivor is likely to remarry and start a second family. The deceased spouse may have desired that whatever property he or she provided for the survivor be for the benefit of the survivor for his or her lifetime and ultimately pass to the children of the first marriage. The Q-TIP trust ensures those wishes will be carried out.

Let us pause now to evaluate our financial stereo system and see what benefits it provides the family and its members. We now have six components—*two* wills and *four* trusts—and the basic system. As we shall see, what we have created is capable of producing some rather sophisticated financial and estate planning results.

Orientation Period

Personal Financial Life Cycle

Age   36–44 Years Old

Income $60,000–$79,000/Year

Net Worth $100,000–$250,000

Life Insurance $600,000–$800,000

Estate Size $700,000–$1,050,000

Estate Systems to Consider

- Wills for both Husband and Wife

- Revocable Living Trust

- Bypass Trust

- Marital Trust

- Qualified Terminal Interest Trust or "Q-TIP"

CHART 10.8

Marital Trust

- Funded for Convenience of Survivor

- Survivor's Property

- Survivor Has Total Control Over Assets

CHART 10.9

172

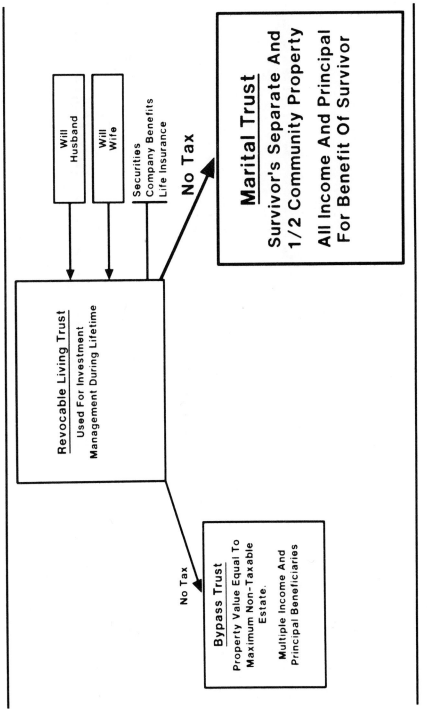

Will
Husband

Will
Wife

Securities
Company Benefits
Life Insurance

Revocable Living Trust
Used For Investment
Management During Lifetime

No Tax

Marital Trust
Survivor's Separate And
1/2 Community Property

All Income And Principal
For Benefit Of Survivor

No Tax

Bypass Trust
Property Value Equal To
Maximum Non-Taxable
Estate.

Multiple Income And
Principal Beneficiaries

CHART 10.10

QTIP Trust

- Funded With Any Portion of the Unlimited Marital Deduction Property

- 100% of Income to Survivor During their Lifetime

- Disposition According to Decedent's Will

CHART 10.11

174

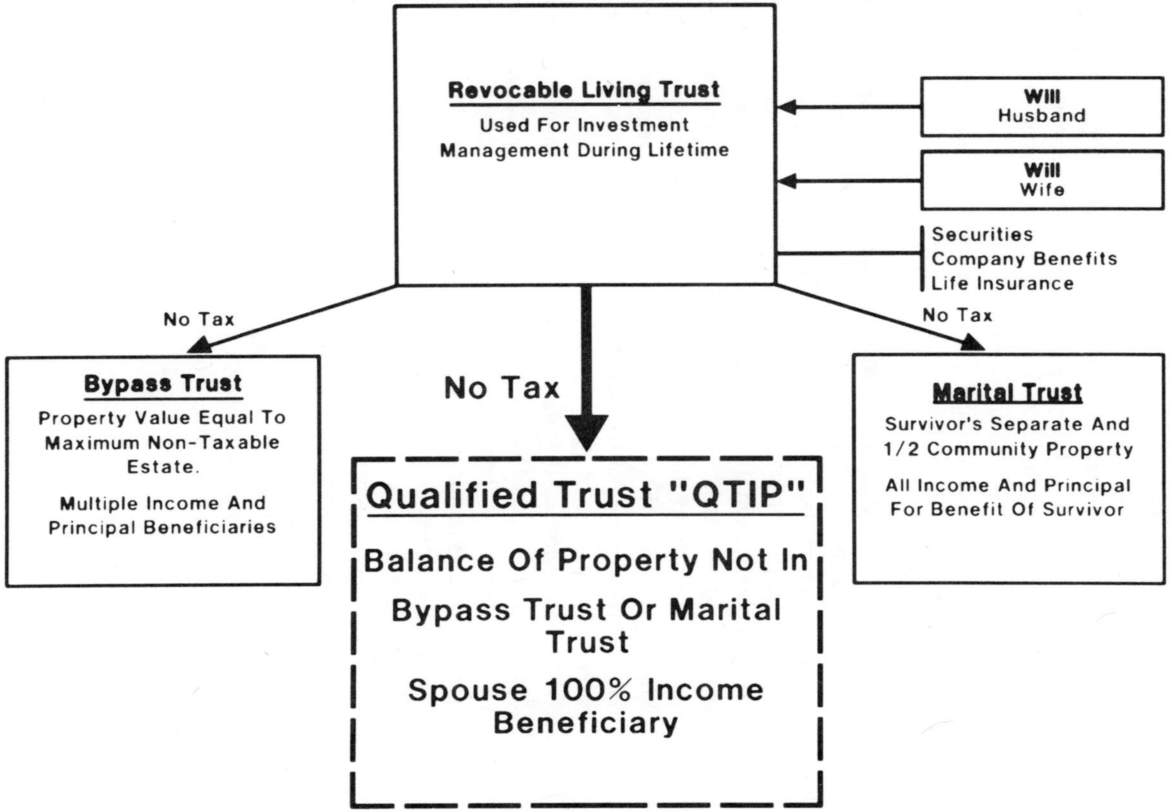

Will
Husband

Will
Wife

Securities
Company Benefits
Life Insurance

No Tax

Revocable Living Trust
Used For Investment
Management During Lifetime

Marital Trust
Survivor's Separate And
1/2 Community Property

All Income And Principal
For Benefit Of Survivor

No Tax

Qualified Trust "QTIP"

Balance Of Property Not In
Bypass Trust Or Marital
Trust

Spouse 100% Income
Beneficiary

No Tax

Bypass Trust
Property Value Equal To
Maximum Non-Taxable
Estate.

Multiple Income And
Principal Beneficiaries

CHART 10.12

We have created, as distributions from the Revocable Living Trust upon the death of the first spouse, *three* trusts: *one* Bypass Trust, *one* Marital Trust and *one* Qualified Terminal Interest Trust. In the process, we have also created a dandy shelter for the surviving spouse and the children. It is a tax shelter, to be sure, but not the type of tax shelters referred to in the Preface.

No tax becomes due under this program when the first spouse dies. This tax-free transfer results from the dual features of the unlimited marital deduction and the lifetime transfer tax exemption.

If both Mary and John should die during this period, the Bypass Trust will pass property-tax free to the children and grandchildren as John and Mary intended. (Chart 10.13)

The Q-TIP and the Marital Trusts will be subject to regular transfer tax assessments, less the survivor's lifetime transfer tax exemption of $600,000. The maximum exemption comes into effect in 1987.

If John and Mary Doe have agreed on the distribution of their property, and certainly they should, and if they both die although not at the same time and the surviving spouse has not made adequate provisions, then one-fourth of the estate goes directly to the son and one-fourth to the daughter. One-fourth remains in trust for the children of the son and the remaining one-fourth in trust for the children of the daughter or until the respective grandchildren reach 25 to 30 years of age.

Care should be exercised that distributions of property not be made to minor children. John and Mary Doe, being careful people, have therefore created trusts for the benefit of their grandchildren which terminate *after* the grandchildren reach their majority. It is also not wise to include distributions of significant sums of money to grandchildren before they are grown. To do otherwise often lessens or takes away completely the main disciplinary tool— the financial one—which parents have and need while children are growing up and completing their educations. Also, grandparents should consider parents' wishes.

It is when the children are growing up, especially during their school and college years, that John and Mary Doe (They are alive again!) are moving into the period when demands on their resources are the greatest—The Survival Period. (Chart 10.14)

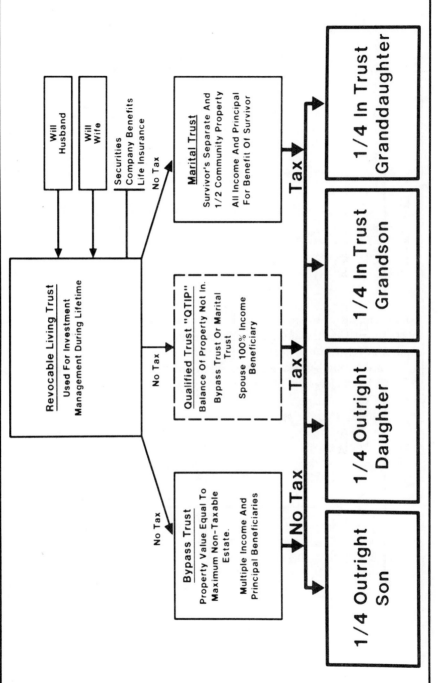

Will
Husband

Will
Wife

Securities
Company Benefits
Life Insurance

No Tax

Revocable Living Trust
Used For Investment
Management During Lifetime

No Tax

No Tax

Bypass Trust
Property Value Equal To
Maximum Non-Taxable
Estate.

Multiple Income And
Principal Beneficiaries

Qualified Trust "QTIP"
Balance Of Property Not In.
Bypass Trust Or Marital
Trust

Spouse 100% Income
Beneficiary

Marital Trust
Survivor's Separate And
1/2 Community Property

All Income And Principal
For Benefit Of Survivor

Tax

No Tax

Tax

Tax

1/4 Outright
Son

1/4 Outright
Daughter

1/4 In Trust
Grandson

1/4 In Trust
Granddaughter

CHART 10.13

177

Kanaly Trust Company

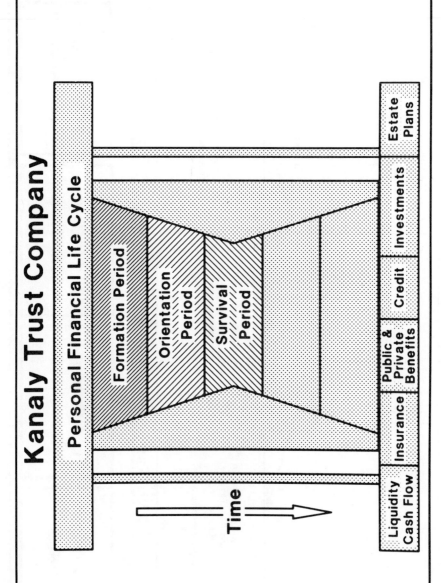

CHART 10.14

THE SURVIVAL PERIOD

For John and Mary Doe this is the period of financial survival—the tight cash-flow period. (Chart 10.15) The time in their Personal Financial Life Cycles when resources are most severely strained and planning must be more effective than ever. The numbers in their family picture are larger. Demands have also increased as illustrated:

The Clifford Trust

We can assume that one of the principal financial burdens John and Mary must carry during the most restrictive hourglass period, if not *the* principal one, is the cost of educating their children. Therefore, in addition to keeping all preceding six components of their financial stereo system in place, the Does must consider adding yet another component: The Clifford Trust. (Chart 10.16 and 10.17)

The primary purpose of the Clifford Trust is to provide funds for education, (a) without disturbing other elements of the financial plan, and (b) at a significantly lower net after-tax cost than if the parents were to pay school and college costs directly. Here's how it works.

John and Mary set up a Clifford Trust and assign certain assets to the trust. These assets must remain in the trust for a period of 10 years or for the life of the grantors or the life of the beneficiaries, whichever is shorter.

Where do the assets for the Clifford Trust come from without disturbing other assets? Answer: they are borrowed. Assuming John and Mary have maintained good liquidity, kept their credit flexible and adequately controlled their cash flow they will be able to borrow money to fund the Clifford Trust. They use money that would have been spent for educational purposes to retire the indebtedness during the 10-year life of the trust.

Income from the trust amounts to a transfer of assets to the Does' children without either significant income tax or transfer tax liabilities. The income could be used for educational purposes for the grandchildren or it could be used for other purposes such as helping aging parents or other family dependents through an Irrevocable Accumulation Trust.

Obviously, the savings of income tax on funds distributed to the children help defray the cost of the loan. It is possible to amortize the loan over the period of the trust. This provides a forced accumulation program of capital for the trust during the 10-year period of the trust's life. In effect, the Clifford Trust provides a means of enabling John and Mary Doe to pay the cost of educating their children with *pre-tax* income.

Assuming that John and Mary live through the Survival Period, and most Johns and Marys do despite all the financial and psychological pressures, they move on to the Accumulation Period of their Personal Financial Life Cycle. (Chart 10.18)

Survival Period

Personal Financial Life Cycle

Age	45–55 Years Old
Income	$80,000–$100,000
Net Worth	$250,000–$500,000
Life Insurance	$800,000–$1,000,000
Estate Size	$1,050,000–$1,500,000

Estate Systems to Consider

- Wills for both Husband and Wife
- Revocable Living Trust
- Bypass Trust
- Q-TIP Trust
- Marital Trust
- Clifford Trust

CHART 10.15

Clifford Trust

- Grantor Assigns Assets to Trust

- Generally Assets Must Stay in Trust for Ten Years

- Designed to Transfer Income to Lower Tax Brackets

CHART 10.16

181

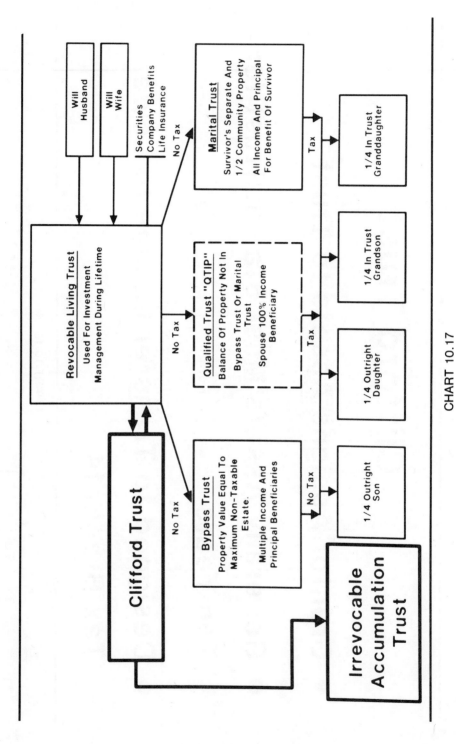

Will Husband

Will Wife

Securities
Company Benefits
Life Insurance

Revocable Living Trust
Used For Investment
Management During Lifetime

No Tax

Marital Trust
Survivor's Separate And
1/2 Community Property

All Income And Principal
For Benefit Of Survivor

Tax

1/4 In Trust
Granddaughter

No Tax

Qualified Trust "QTIP"
Balance Of Property Not In
Bypass Trust Or Marital
Trust

Spouse 100% Income
Beneficiary

Tax

1/4 In Trust
Grandson

1/4 Outright
Daughter

Clifford Trust

No Tax

Bypass Trust
Property Value Equal To
Maximum Non-Taxable
Estate.

Multiple Income And
Principal Beneficiaries

No Tax

1/4 Outright
Son

Irrevocable Accumulation Trust

CHART 10.17

182

Kanaly Trust Company

Personal Financial Life Cycle

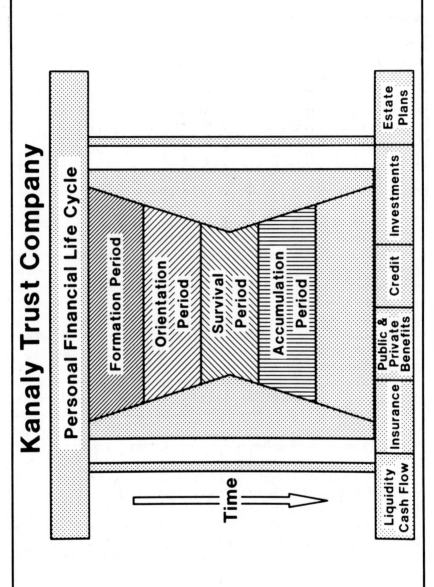

Formation Period

Orientation Period

Survival Period

Accumulation Period

Time

Liquidity Cash Flow | Insurance | Public & Private Benefits | Credit | Investments | Estate Plans

CHART 10.18

THE ACCUMULATION PERIOD

John and Mary are now middle-aged. Educational expenses, at least the bulk of them, have been met thanks in large part to the Clifford Trust. Their life-style is pleasant and satisfying and is characterized by their having adequate funds and leisure time to do many of the things they've always wanted to do. Their "numbers" are impressive and financially they look something like this: (Chart 10.19)

All of the preceding components of their financial stereo system continue in place, including the education-oriented Clifford Trust designed to provide income for their children and/or educational funds for their grandchildren.

The Irrevocable Life Insurance Trust

John and Mary are now in a position for the first time in their lives to consider ways to reduce their estate in order to minimize tax exposure. The method most generally employed in this phase of their Personal Financial Life Cycle is the Irrevocable Life Insurance Trust. (Chart 10.20 and 10.21)

In such a trust all or part of John's and Mary's life insurance ownership interest is assigned to an irrevocable trust, thereby removing the proceeds of the insurance from their taxable estates. Although irrevocable, the trust should include a provision permitting the trustee to buy assets from or lend money to John or Mary Doe's estate. The reason: to enable the executors to pay estate debts and taxes with the proceeds of life insurance. The insurance payable to the trust is not subject to claims or creditors and remains a part of the private lives of the Doe family and estate.

Generally speaking, the surviving spouse may be the beneficiary of the trust, that is, if the life insurance is the separate property of the insured donor. If the insurance is community property, then most likely only one-half of the proceeds of the life insurance can be included in the beneficial usage of the surviving spouse. The remainder may go to the children or other persons or entities.

The premiums paid for life insurance in the insurance trust can be used as a part of the annual gift exclusion provided for under tax law.

As you will recall, it is during this period that people normally experience the most rapid accumulation of assets. So it is in the case of the Does. Their lifestyle remains relatively stable, but as a rule their income continues to increase. Even if their income remains stable and outgo decreases they can use any surplus funds for a better lifestyle or to invest. This is the phase of the Personal Life Cycle in which accumulation of investment-type assets is most important.

Inevitably, the accumulation of assets is followed by distribution. Distribution should be a planned, orderly process taking place during the fifth and last phase of the Personal Financial Life Cycle—the Preservation Period. (Chart 10.22)

Accumulation Period

Personal Financial Life Cycle

Age	55–65 Years Old
Income	$100,000–$200,000
Net Worth	$500,000–$1,000,000
Life Insurance	$1,000,000–$2,000,000
Estate Size	$1,500,000–$3,000,000

Estate Systems to Consider

- Wills for both Husband and Wife
- Revocable Living Trust
- Bypass Trust
- Q-TIP Trust
- Marital Trust
- Clifford Trust
- Irrevocable Life Insurance Trust

CHART 10.19

Irrevocable Life Insurance Trust

- Irrevocably Assign Insurance

- Removes Proceeds From Estate

- Trust Can Buy Assets From or Lend Money to the Estate

- Not Subject to Claims of Creditors

CHART 10.20

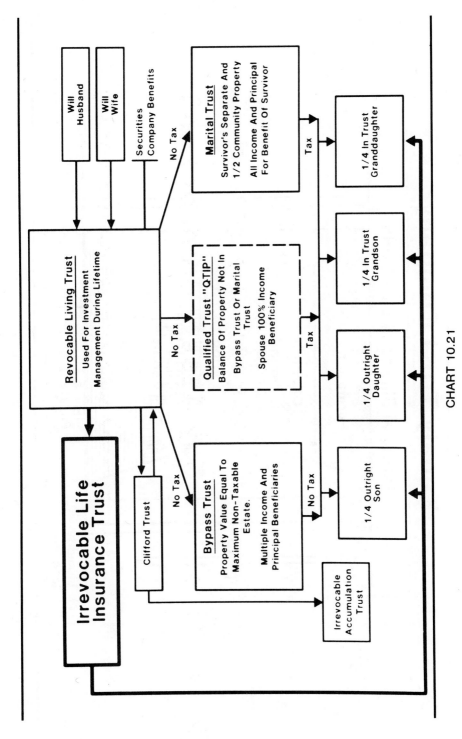

CHART 10.21

Will Husband

Will Wife

Securities
Company Benefits

No Tax

Marital Trust
Survivor's Separate And
1/2 Community Property

All Income And Principal
For Benefit Of Survivor

Revocable Living Trust
Used For Investment
Management During Lifetime

No Tax

Qualified Trust "QTIP"
Balance Of Property Not In
Bypass Trust Or Marital
Trust

Spouse 100% Income
Beneficiary

No Tax

Clifford Trust

Bypass Trust
Property Value Equal To
Maximum Non-Taxable
Estate.

Multiple Income And
Principal Beneficiaries

**Irrevocable Life
Insurance Trust**

Irrevocable
Accumulation
Trust

Tax

1/4 In Trust
Granddaughter

Tax

1/4 In Trust
Grandson

Tax

1/4 Outright
Daughter

No Tax

1/4 Outright
Son

Kanaly Trust Company

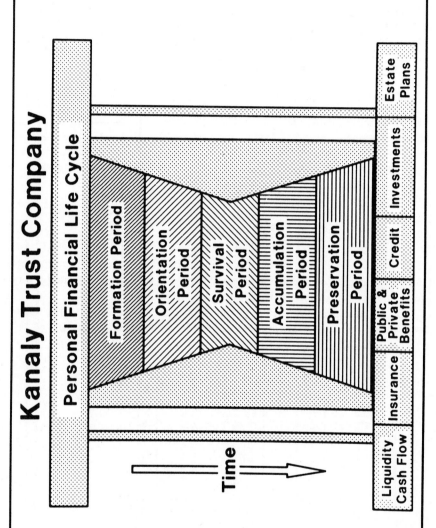

Personal Financial Life Cycle

Formation Period
Orientation Period
Survival Period
Accumulation Period
Preservation Period

Time

Liquidity Cash Flow
Insurance
Public & Private Benefits
Credit
Investments
Estate Plans

CHART 10.22

188

THE PRESERVATION PERIOD

As John and Mary Doe move into the Preservation Period their financial vital statistics are quite large (Chart 10.23):

During the Preservation Period there are many financial planning options available to John and Mary Doe for distribution of their assets. I will cover four of the more important and commonly exercised ones. They are the Charitable Lead Trust, the Charitable Remainder Unitrust, the Individual Retirement Account (IRA) Rollover and the Family Corporation.

The Charitable Lead Trust

The Charitable Lead Trust is a trust in which John and Mary may place certain accumulated assets which they believe are likely to appreciate substantially. (Chart 10.24 and 10.25) They may so design the trust to specify that the income from this trust go directly to the charity or charities they designate. The beneficiaries may be changed during the life of the trust by the Does. The trust will terminate at the designated ages of their children or grandchildren or after a specific number of years. The present value of the assets for transfer tax purposes will be reduced by the extent of the charitable distributions made during the life of the trust.

The Does will earn a tax deduction each year based on the amounts given to charity. However the trust may generally be designed in such a way that little or no transfer tax is required.

If the trust doubles, triples or quadruples in value during its life, whatever remains passes to the children or grandchildren or other designated beneficiaries *tax-free*. Since the transfer tax now is a unified tax, i.e., no distinction is made between lifetime gifts and testamentary dispositions, it is important that the Does consider giving property to the trust which will probably appreciate. They may satisfy their charitable requirements on an annual basis through gifts of income from the trust.

The appreciation of the trust assets may become a substantial asset passing to the family, possibly without transfer tax liability.

Preservation Period
Personal Financial Life Cycle

Age   66 Years and beyond
Income $150,000–$250,000/year
Net Worth $1,000,000–$2,000,000
Life Insurance $450,000–$900,000
Estate Size $1,450,000–$2,900,000

Estate Systems to Consider

- Wills for both Husband and Wife
- Revocable Living Trust
- Bypass Trust
- Q-TIP Trust
- Marital Trust
- Clifford Trust
- Irrevocable Life Insurance Trust
- Charitable Lead Trust
- Charitable Remainder Unitrust
- Individual Retirement Account—Rollover
- Family Corporation

CHART 10.23

Charitable Lead Trust

- Can Be Designed So That No Transfer Tax is Paid

- Grantor Receives Deduction for Income Given to Charity

- Appreciated Remainder Goes to Children or Grandchildren

CHART 10.24

191

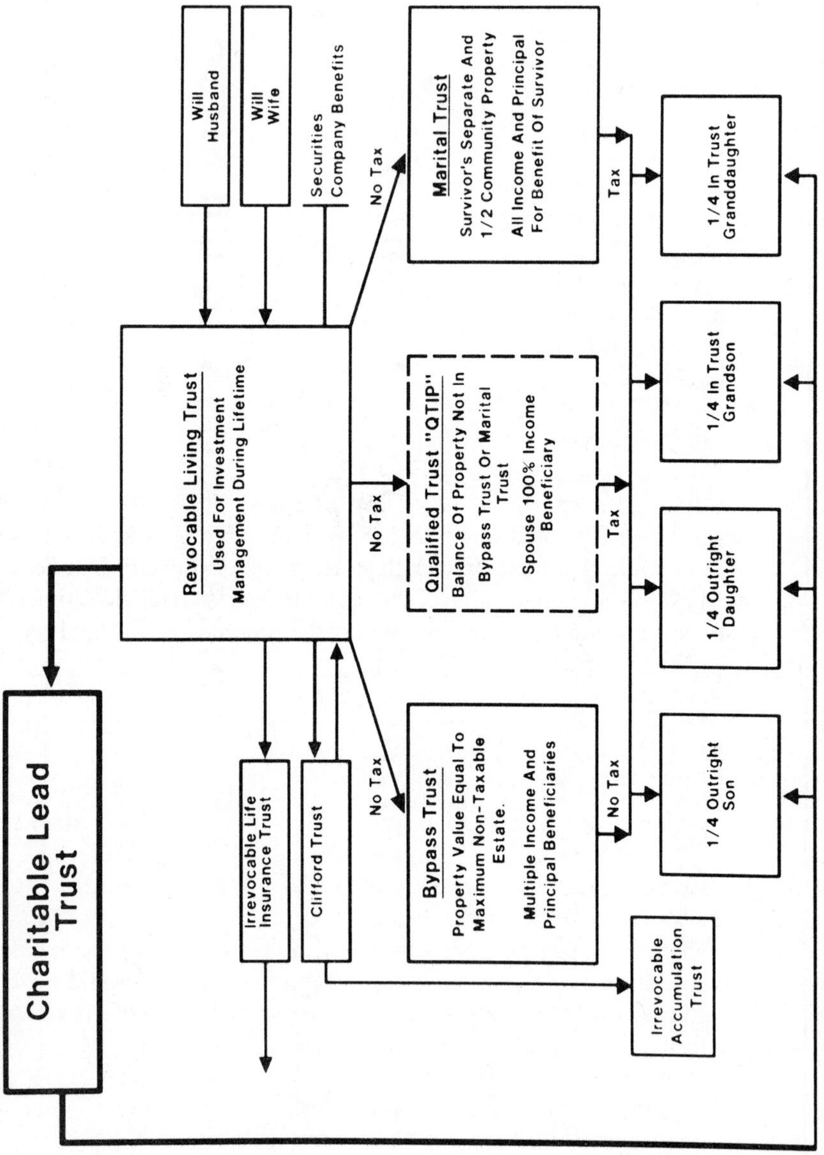

Will
Husband

Will
Wife

Securities
Company Benefits

No Tax

Revocable Living Trust
Used For Investment
Management During Lifetime

Charitable Lead
Trust

Irrevocable Life
Insurance Trust

Clifford Trust

No Tax

No Tax

Marital Trust
Survivor's Separate And
1/2 Community Property
All Income And Principal
For Benefit Of Survivor

Qualified Trust "QTIP"
Balance Of Property Not In
Bypass Trust Or Marital
Trust
Spouse 100% Income
Beneficiary

Bypass Trust
Property Value Equal To
Maximum Non-Taxable
Estate.
Multiple Income And
Principal Beneficiaries

Irrevocable
Accumulation
Trust

Tax

Tax

No Tax

1/4 In Trust
Granddaughter

1/4 In Trust
Grandson

1/4 Outright
Daughter

1/4 Outright
Son

CHART 10.25

192

The Charitable Remainder Unitrust

At this point John and Mary may also consider a financial planning tool known as the Charitable Remainder Unitrust. (Chart 10.26 and 10.27) This is a vehicle through which the Does may transfer appreciated assets such as stock or real estate in which they have a low-cost base and substantial appreciation based on current market values.

The Charitable Remainder Unitrust does not trigger a capital gains tax when the asset is sold because the remainder interest is considered a charitable gift and therefore tax free.

The Does receive an immediate income tax deduction for the present value of the future gift based on their actuarial life expectancy at the time of the transfer.

There would be no transfer tax at either John's or Mary's death inasmuch as the property passes, after the second death, to the charities designated at the time of the gift.

The designated charities may be changed by the Does at any time during the life of the trust.

John and Mary may receive an income from the assets in trust during the life of the trust. Income may be stated in terms of an annual dollar amount. In this case the trust is known as a Charitable Annuity Trust. If the income is stated as a percentage of the market value of the trust it is known as a Charitable Remainder Unitrust. In our illustration John and Mary Doe keep the income of 8% of the market value of the trust for their individual lifetimes. At the Does' passing the trust terminates and the proceeds go to the designated charity or charities.

The Charitable Remainder Unitrust combines the features of substantial income tax savings, the avoidance of capital gains taxes and the avoidance of transfer tax. As demonstrated in the foregoing illustration the Charitable Remainder Unitrust frequently results in tax savings for the family almost equal to the value of the assets transferred to the trust. That is, the estate without the Charitable Remainder Unitrust would have been reduced by as much by resulting taxes as it was by the value of the gift to the trust.

But there's more to this approximate financial washout. We must add the income which John and Mary received from their 8% share of the assets plus the savings of any taxes, income and/or capital gains they would have had to pay had they used the assets for income production instead of assigning those assets to the Charitable Remainder Unitrust.

The trust must last for twenty years unless the beneficiaries of the trust die before the end of the twenty year period, in which case the trust ends at the death of the last surviving beneficiary.

Now it is time to take another look at our financial stereo system. What additional benefits or results is it producing for John and Mary Doe?

First, the system has enabled the Does to plan and satisfy their annual charitable donations.

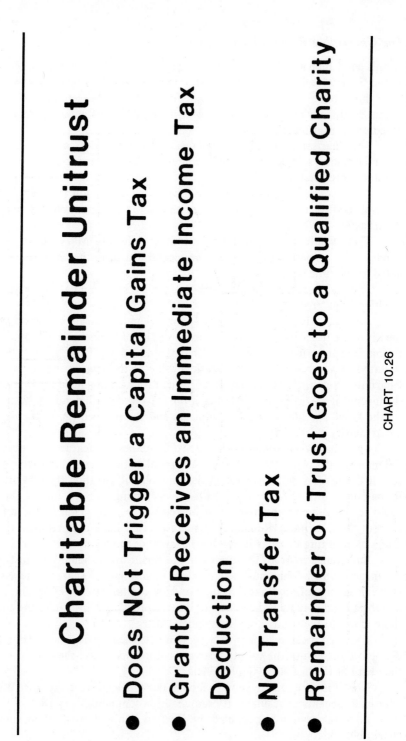

Charitable Remainder Unitrust

- Does Not Trigger a Capital Gains Tax

- Grantor Receives an Immediate Income Tax Deduction

- No Transfer Tax

- Remainder of Trust Goes to a Qualified Charity

CHART 10.26

194

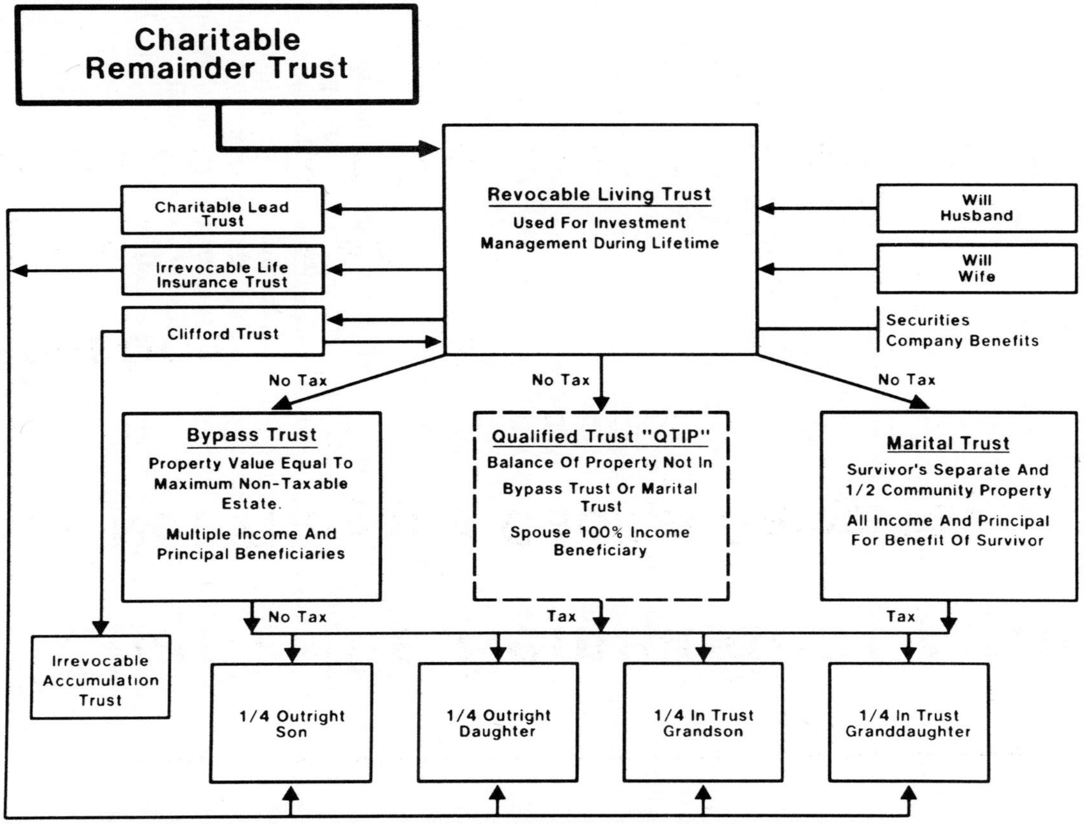

CHART 10.27

Charitable Remainder Trust

Will Husband

Will Wife

Securities Company Benefits

No Tax

Revocable Living Trust
Used For Investment Management During Lifetime

Marital Trust
Survivor's Separate And 1/2 Community Property
All Income And Principal For Benefit Of Survivor

No Tax

Qualified Trust "QTIP"
Balance Of Property Not In Bypass Trust Or Marital Trust
Spouse 100% Income Beneficiary

No Tax

Charitable Lead Trust

Irrevocable Life Insurance Trust

Clifford Trust

No Tax

Bypass Trust
Property Value Equal To Maximum Non-Taxable Estate.
Multiple Income And Principal Beneficiaries

Irrevocable Accumulation Trust

Tax

Tax

No Tax

1/4 In Trust Granddaughter

1/4 In Trust Grandson

1/4 Outright Daughter

1/4 Outright Son

195

Second, the use of the Charitable Lead Trust has enabled them to begin the orderly and tax-advantaged transfer of assets to their children and grandchildren.

Finally, they have been able to contribute to the community at large or to their favorite charities while simultaneously enhancing their incomes during their lifetimes. This feat is accomplished through the use of the Charitable Remainder Trust.

All in all, our financial stereo system seems to be producing some very sweet and dynamic music for John and Mary.

The Individual Retirement Account (IRA) Rollover

If the Does are participating in a qualified benefit plan (pension, savings, profit sharing, salary deferral or stock purchase), or have participated in one during their working years, they may now be eligible for what is termed an Individual Retirement Account (IRA) Rollover. (Chart 10.28 and 10.29)

The IRA Rollover is simply a trust funded with a lump sum of money from *any* qualified plan. The amount is generally that which has accumulated in the various plans at the time of retirement, less of course, John's and Mary's contributions. All earnings in the IRA Rollover will accumulate tax-free while in the fund. Distribution may begin at age 59 years 6 months but must commence by age 70 years 6 months under current law. Distributions must be withdrawn over the actuarial life expectancy of John and Mary Doe. The distributions when taken are subject to ordinary income taxes at the levels then payable by John and Mary. You will recall the $600,000 maximum occurs after 1987. So they will have additional income sources later in life from the IRA Rollover, including the money accumulated in their thrift savings, profit sharing or pension plan while employed.

John and Mary Doe have done an excellent job of securing their futures, while at the same time passing on certain properties, life insurance proceeds and other valuable assets to their children and grandchildren. They have provided for their own income and lifestyle needs through the various financial planning components they have been constructing. It is important that John and Mary Doe continue living and doing the many things they enjoy. Never overlook the probability of a long life and the need to plan for a possible 100-year life expectancy. That, in turn, means one or both of the Does will likely be engaged in more than one career.

IRA Rollover

- Funded With Savings Plan Assets at Retirement (Less Executive's Contributions)

- All Earnings Accumulate Tax-Deferred

- Distribution May Begin at Age 59 1/2 And Must Begin at Age 70 1/2

- Distributions Subject to Ordinary Income Tax

CHART 10.28

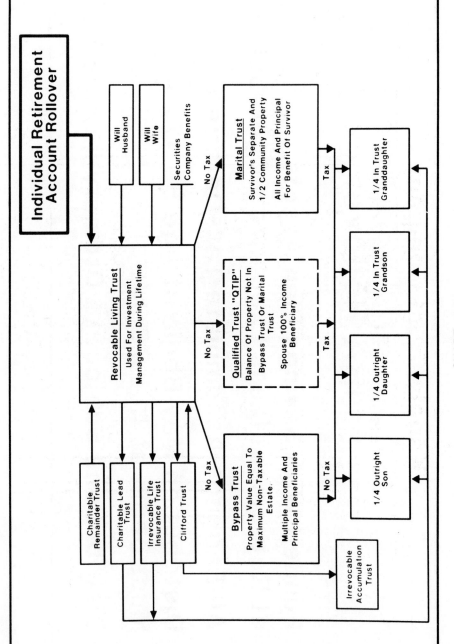

Individual Retirement Account Rollover

Will Husband

Will Wife

Securities Company Benefits

No Tax

Marital Trust
Survivor's Separate And 1/2 Community Property All Income And Principal For Benefit Of Survivor

Revocable Living Trust
Used For Investment Management During Lifetime

No Tax

Qualified Trust "QTIP"
Balance Of Property Not In Bypass Trust Or Marital Trust
Spouse 100% Income Beneficiary

No Tax

Charitable Remainder Trust

Charitable Lead Trust

Irrevocable Life Insurance Trust

Clifford Trust

No Tax

Bypass Trust
Property Value Equal To Maximum Non-Taxable Estate.
Multiple Income And Principal Beneficiaries

Irrevocable Accumulation Trust

Tax

1/4 In Trust Granddaughter

1/4 In Trust Grandson

Tax

1/4 Outright Daughter

No Tax

1/4 Outright Son

CHART 10.29

198

The Family Corporation

Both John and Mary Doe are now in a position, personally and financially, to seek and accept new career and business opportunities. Frequently the Family Corporation becomes an important, even indispensable, financial and estate planning device for people in the Does' position. (Chart 10.30 and 10.31)

The Family Corporation's value lies in the fact that it separates business risk from investment risk thereby insulating the family's personal wealth from further risk-taking or venture capital activities. As such, the Family Corporation can be thought of as a capital preservation tool.

And the corporation offers tax benefits as well. Only 15% of investment income, derived by the Family Corporation in the form of dividends from common or preferred stocks of other companies is taxed. That is, only 15% of dividends received by one corporation from another are subject to federal income tax at the corporate level. So we can reduce the family's taxable income from dividends by transferring stock to a Family Corporation. The earnings in the Family Corporation are usually generated at a lower income tax rate, and the corporation may retain earnings tax-free up to certain limits. A Family Corporation may also provide benefits such as office facilities, salaries and pensions, and thrift and savings programs for employee family members as well as for the corporation's non-family employees.

In order to avoid the personal holding-company tax, which is an excess profits tax, John and Mary Doe must be able to show that at least 40% of the gross of the Family Corporation's revenues come from business-related activities; that is, if their corporation actually makes a profit. Business-related revenue in a Family Corporation usually includes income from oil and gas, working interests, farm and ranch operations and consulting fees earned by John or Mary, provided such fees are payable to the corporation.

The remaining 60% may come from passive investment income such as stocks, bonds, real estate or other securities transferred to the corporation or owned by it as a result of the investing of accumulated earnings.

Not the least of the values of a Family Corporation is that it provides psychic as well as financial income. The family has an opportunity to continue doing things they enjoy doing or take up new challenges without the concommitant risks. For most of us tolerance for risk declines as we grow older, and a Family Corporation addresses that circumstance quite nicely.

Another potential benefit: John and Mary Doe can create subsidiary corporations to enable their children to get a financial start in business or the professions. Certain types of stock may be used to permit the parent corporation or family corporation to charge off the loss of the subsidiaries against ordinary income as opposed to capital loss. An option may be given to the children or participating stockholders in the subsidiary to buy the subsidiary corporation once the business is profitable. In the meantime, consolidating the earnings of the subsidiary and the family corporation permit losses to be taken against income in the parent corporation. A Family Corporation can become a gold mine of tax benefits.

Family Corporation

- Separates Business Risk From Investment Risk So That One's Personal Wealth Is Insulated

- Dividend Income Receives 85% Tax Exclusion

- Generate Earnings At Lower Income Tax Rates And The Corporation May Retain Earnings Tax–Free, Up To Certain Limits

CHART 10.30

Family Corporation

- Individual Retirement Account Rollover
- Will Husband
- Will Wife
- Securities Company Benefits

Revocable Living Trust
Used For Investment Management During Lifetime

- Charitable Remainder Trust
- Charitable Lead Trust
- Irrevocable Life Insurance Trust
- Clifford Trust

No Tax

Marital Trust
Survivor's Separate And 1/2 Community Property All Income And Principal For Benefit Of Survivor

No Tax

Qualified Trust "QTIP"
Balance Of Property Not In Bypass Trust Or Marital Trust
Spouse 100% Income Beneficiary

No Tax

Bypass Trust
Property Value Equal To Maximum Non-Taxable Estate.
Multiple Income And Principal Beneficiaries

No Tax

Irrevocable Accumulation Trust

Tax

- 1/4 In Trust Granddaughter
- 1/4 In Trust Grandson
- 1/4 Outright Daughter
- 1/4 Outright Son

CHART 10.31

201

ROBERTS FAMILY, INC.

Over the years we have assisted many clients in establishing their own family corporations. These clients have experienced very satisfactory results from the ownership and use of these privately held units. This brief story about the Roberts family corporation serves well to make the point. (The names have been changed, but the case is factual.)

Mr. Roberts was the executive-owner of a Houston corporation. Over a period of time the Roberts family had developed an interest in ranching. The city-bound family derived a great deal of pleasure from vacationing at dude ranches and spending time in the country. The youngsters enjoyed horseback riding, and Mrs. Roberts, who'd spent her early years on a large cattle ranch in a western state, missed the lifestyle she remembered so fondly from her childhood.

The Roberts had accumulated a portfolio of stocks and owned a substantial equity in a large Houston home. Mr. Roberts had been self-employed for more than fifteen years. He was covered by a generous pension and profit sharing plan at his family-owned company. The family had developed a sound financial plan a dozen years before and had systematically up-dated and fine-tuned the plan. They had come to the point when they wanted to own their own ranch.

We assisted them in purchasing a large cattle ranch about 200 miles from Houston. We turned the ranch into an operating corporation with the stock in the ranch corporation held by the Roberts family. A major portion of the funds used to acquire the ranch came from a local bank. Cash, in the form of dividends from common stock transferred to the corporation, flowed to the family corporation at an attractive corporate income tax rate. The dividends helped the family corporation retire much of the bank loan. Income from the ranch was available for improvements. Next, we set up tax-favored benefit plans at the ranch corporation for the benefit of family employees involved in the operation and management of the property. The ranch corporation provided automobiles and other legitimate fringe benefits.

Ownership of the ranch itself was systematically transferred from the parents to the children through a series of preferred and common stock. Preferred stock was distributed to Mr. and Mrs. Roberts with common stock going to the children. This accomplishes a partial estate freeze through the distribution of two classes of stock. Through individual shares the property remained intact and undivided. One member of the family was able to transfer his or her interests to other members without affecting the property as a whole. Ownership could be passed from generation to generation while maintaining the ranch unaltered. Restriction of the ranch corporation shares was designed to ensure the stock ownership would remain only in the hands of family members. This was accomplished through buy-and-sell agreements.

This form of financial planning is versatile and allowed the family numerous options. If they should decide to sell the ranch to an outside party, this is easily accomplished. They could sell a portion of the land or lease all or part of the property to third parties. Through the ranch corporation, added properties could be acquired. The opportunities are truly unlimited.

As the Roberts family can testify, the family corporation is probably one of today's best tax shelters, especially for a family unit. It is one of the most overlooked opportunities for progressive family financial planning which may benefit several generations.

Concluding Observations

The keys to understanding, accumulating, preserving and enjoying wealth are numerous. I believe fundamentally in the old adage of using the "kiss" method: "*keep it simple, stupid*." My experience indicates people often tend to unnecessarily complicate their personal financial lives. They are so busy making money they have little time remaining to figure out what to do with it. Statistics indicate about 3,000 hours are spent each year by each of us creating income and only ten hours, on the average, planning what to do with the things income makes possible.

This is due to the fact America is still a frontier nation. There seems to always be more out there, more land, more timber, more water—then more economic opportunity from agriculture and from industry. Now we are in the post-industrial or an information and services society. The same frontier mentality exists. There's always more out there. Civilizations which have endured longer than ours have learned to make do with finite territory, limited land, minimal resources and fewer socio-economic opportunities. Today there is more waste of personal finance resources than there ever has been in misspent energy and wasted resource consumption in the history of this country. We can and must regain our productivity and capital formation capabilities which have been the chief forces thrusting our country into the forefront of the free world.

To do that we must learn to get more out of all resources: land, mineral resources and, of course, our personal financial resources. Information in this book provides an incentive and, hopefully, desire to take steps leading to a better understanding of accumulating, preserving and enjoying our property to its fullest. The book deals primarily with matters attributable to accumulating and preserving our wealth. It also provides a better understanding of wealth, per se, and the steps necessary to take toward enjoying wealth. The two are certainly correlated. When we learn to think of the two as one function we are on our way to simplifying our lives.

It is only when we fully understand wealth, in terms of its true meaning to the human being, that we learn how to truly enjoy wealth and its many fruits. The common understanding of wealth in the United States, it seems to me, has been far too much directed toward increasing and enhancing our lifestyles and our standards of living while building of a basis for power, prestige and recognition. To me, these are not worthy objectives.

My experience indicates that the assimilation of wealth for lifestyle improvement will probably always be with us but to varying degrees of importance, especially for new generations. Who among the well-to-do has not found that material possessions are relatively unimportant once acquired? Why do suicides occur more often among the wealthy than among those living in the ghettos?

I am realistic and recognize human nature is not likely to change sufficiently to preclude the use of wealth for obtaining power, prestige and recognition. This aspect of wealth and the desire for wealth will be around forever; I am certain of this human trait surviving beyond our present economic systems.

I do submit for your reasoning and consideration three additional factors for aiding in the understanding of wealth. Recognizing and understanding this trinity will lead toward a higher degree of enjoying wealth once it has been achieved.

First, wealth and private ownership afford the individual the right of privacy without which government, individuals and institutions would likely intrude to an even greater degree than is the case today. Private property enables the individual to think, live and participate in the community in a more personalized and secure manner than if private ownership were impossible. Consider the miserable lifestyles of those living in countries where private ownership is banned.

Second, wealth provides a freedom to the individual to pursue varying career vocations without being involved in the necessity of earning a daily wage, freedom to choose the things we like, the places we want to go, the activities in which we participate. And don't overlook educational pursuits made possible by wealth. Without private property or wealth such worthy pursuits would not be available to most.

Our accumulations provide us with integrity in our voting and political affiliations, in our charitable activities and community involvements. Freedom to be ourselves, to think our thoughts, to relate more properly to the sensitivity of others, to be concerned about others and for others as opposed to serving self-interests only—these are among the valuable products and by-products of private property.

And third, private ownership of property and wealth enables one to achieve a sense of security and well-being that's not generally obtainable through other human institutions, security in the sense of knowing one can take care of oneself while recognizing interdependence with others. We can nonetheless be certain we are not encroaching on rights of others by acquiring or maintaining a sense of security that is not dependent upon others, be it government, individual or family. Security enables one to dream dreams, seek new careers, explore new worlds, be compassionate, be empathetic of our fellow family members and be more creative and constructive in our interpersonal relations.

Everyone wants to have some "to-hell-with-you" money. My experience indicates that once we get it, and the amount varies with each of us, we don't really need mad money for the purposes of independence. We have our zone of privacy. We're free to think and act and create. We are secure in the knowledge that we will not be an imposition on others (including ourselves) through all the big exigencies of life as discussed earlier in this book. An understanding of these factors of wealth should lead one to a genuine peace of mind and enable one to fully enjoy wealth more constructively than may have been the case in the past.

Our entire socio-economic-political system seems to suggest we should feel guilty if we have accumulated a nice income or discretionary assets over and above life's basic needs. I resent this obligation to take a needless guilt trip. It's okay for people to have become self-sufficient. It's okay to have nicer things. It's okay to enjoy a qualitative as well as quantitative life. It's okay to be able to share our assets with others without feeling like self-deprivation. It's okay to be able to police government, educational and business institutions more carefully because of greater freedom, privacy, security and independence. One should not be intimidated by *demands* of a community, or educational institutions, or government, or charities, or arts, or religion other than what one considers to be his or her *fair contributions* to all of these human institutions.

If we keep our plan simple and provide for good liquidity, know our cash flow and develop a personal financial strategy that identifies and fills our needs; and if we define our investment objectives and develop a strategy to fulfill them as we gradually substitute investment or passive income for vocational income; and if we insure against unexpected losses and take maximum advantage of the benefit plans afforded us; and if we accomplish our estate-planning objectives of providing for the exigencies of life—living too long, dying too soon or incurring disability or impairment, while being empathic about the needs of all of our family members—then, and only then, will we have developed a truly mature fiscal and financial attitude allowing us to mold a successful strategy for each of our individual financial cycles. That's about all we can do. It's a big order but a series of goals worthy of our best efforts.

I'm hopeful that your use of the information provided in this book will make a contribution to your overall financial thinking and will lead you to a simplified method and strategy for developing your own financial plans. The result, I hope sincerely, will be *your* accomplishment of a most enjoyable *life* strategy that will *enable you to work hard, live clean, plod along and save your money.* (This is my wife's favorite statement relating to the ideal life. She has summed it up very nicely.) Most important of all, your plans should allow you to feel satisfaction at *all* stages of your life cycle, knowing you have done the best you can to provide for yourself and your family. That's about all anyone can do. I sincerely hope you achieve the sense of peace that comes from being able to enjoy what you have and know you can actually afford to live like you do. It's a *true* sense of peace, and you can have it.

Most of my clients say they wish they'd known me and my organization twenty years earlier. They wish they'd known of the work we have been doing for the past quarter of a century. One of my clients told me recently, "You know, your financial life cycle has real meaning to me. I spent the first half of my life getting to the point where I could eat what I wanted. Now I'm spending the last half being damned sure I don't!"

We can all afford to live the way we do—indeed, even the way we dream of living. And we can do it with total pleasure and satisfaction—without apologies or feelings of guilt.

I believe this with all my heart, soul and mind. I hope you do, too.

GUIDELINES FOR SELECTING A FINANCIAL COUNSELLOR

Potential Conflict-of-Interest Limitations

- Does the firm own or operate, or is it tied directly or indirectly to, any of the following businesses?
  1. Bank or savings and loan
  2. Insurance brokerage or insurance company
  3. Stock and general securities brokerage or dealer service
  4. Tax shélter or tax-advantaged investments
  5. Accounting firm

      Your professional counsellor should be *totally independent* and not involved or entangled in alliances with other financial companies.

Method of Compensation

- Does the firm derive income by securing commissions from the sale of securities or other financial products (insurance policies, tax shelters, etc.)?
  Your counsellor should not be involved in selling *any* products.
- Does the firm (or any affiliate, subsidiary or related business organization) directly or indirectly receive any finders' commissions, placement commis-

sions or carried interests that supplement or replace the counselling fee itself and thus help support the firm?

Be certain your counsellor is free of conflicts of interest. Use only planning organizations which are paid by *you* for their *advice* and *service,* known as "fee only" counsellors.

Protection of Clients

- How is the firm regulated and audited?
  The firm should be examined by a governmental authority and subject to annual audits by a respected CPA firm.
- What is the extent of the firm's capitalization?
  Your counsellor should be able to show adequate financial responsibility for advice given. Substantial net worth, adequate professional insurance and employee fidelity bonding should be considered.
- Are the firm's employees bonded and covered by liability and fidelity insurance?
- Ask to see documentation and evidence of liability insurance, performance bonds, etc.

Investment Strategy

- How is the firm's investment policy determined?
  Look for organizations whose policy is shaped by a competent, skilled advisory board which meets regularly. The board should represent a wide range of business, academic and civic backgrounds.
- Does the firm make use of pooled-fund investments?
  Avoid counseling organizations where extensive use of pooled-funds exists. Pooled-funds are acceptable only where relatively small accounts are involved.

Administration of the Counselling Process

- How is the financial counselling program actually administered?
  Visit the offices of your potential financial counsellor. Interview the principals and review the systems and procedures.
- What steps are taken to *follow through* on the recommendations in the client's full report?
  When examining your counsellor's procedures be alert for follow-up systems. What are the checks and balances used to ensure proper implementation?
- Is the spouse included in the counselling process?
  Be sure the counsellor is concerned about the financial plan's affect on

the entire family. The counsellor should recommend the spouse be a part of the process.

- Does the firm have the necessary continuity built into it to formulate and implement a multi-generation program?

  Who are the owners and principals? What plans for succession are in place? Know the answers before selecting your firm.

- Is the financial evaluation report customized or is it the product of computer software?

  Every report and prescribed plan should be individualized. Be cautious of counsellors using impersonal off-the-shelf programs or "computerized" plans.

Range of Counselling Services

- In addition to the general financial counselling function are there any specialized services that the firm provides for its individual and company clients?

  Review the total programs available. A complete financial planning service will include these nine functions:
  1. Retirement counselling
  2. Employee-placement counselling
  3. Outplacement counselling
  4. Widow and widower counselling
  5. Expatriate counselling
  6. Tax, investment and economic briefings
  7. "Cafeteria style" or flexible benefits counselling
  8. Business merger/acquisition counselling
  9. Financial counselling seminars tailored for specific groups

Quality and Characteristics of Clients

- What is the firm's client base?

  Ask for client references and details.

- Is the firm familiar with the tax and estate laws of those states and countries where its clients live?

  Ask questions; carefully evaluate responses.

Qualifications of Principals and Staff

- What are the qualifications of the principals and staff? What are their backgrounds?

  Do not assume anything. Interview the professionals who will be working with you. Ask "hard" questions. Verify all information provided.

GLOSSARY OF FREQUENTLY USED FINANCIAL TERMS

Accounting Period   In business an Accounting Period is a period of time over which profits or losses are calculated.

Accrued Interest and Accrued Income   Accrued Interest is interest *due* but not yet paid. Accrued Income is income *earned* but not yet received.

Adjusted Gross Estate   Gross Estate less certain deductions equals the Taxable Estate, another term for the Adjusted Gross Estate.

Administrator   The Administrator is the person or institution appointed by the probate court to settle or administer an estate when there is no will or no executor named. A female administrator is usually known as the Administratrix.

Agent   An agent is a person given authority by another to act in the other person's place or on behalf of another in certain legal or financial matters.

Amortize   Amortize is a term usually associated with paying off a mortgage or debt. To Amortize is to reduce the debt by periodic payment.

Annuity   An Annuity is the regular payment of money for a specified time, usually for life. For example a lifetime annuity pays to the annuitant a stated amount in periodic payments, usually monthly for the life of the annuitant.

Appraise To Appraise property is to place a value on it. In probate proceedings a decedent's estate is appraised by order of the probate court. (See Inventory.)

Appreciation Property Appreciates when it increases in value. This process is called Appreciation, the opposite of depreciation.

Arms Length Transaction An Arms Length Transaction takes place when no prior relationship between buyer and seller has affected any aspect of that sale.

Asset An Asset is something of value owned and therefore available for the payment of debts.

Assign/Assignment To Assign property is to transfer full or partial rights of interest in property to another. An Assignment is the act of such a transfer.

Attest To Attest is to verify the signing of a document. Usually the Attestor signs the document as a witness.

Audit To Audit is to examine financial holdings and transactions.

Basis Basis is an accounting term to identify the cost factor of an investment.

Basis Point One Basis Point is equal to one-hundredth of a percent.

Beneficiary A Beneficiary is a person or other legal entity named to receive income or property. Life insurance contracts specify a Beneficiary to receive the policy proceeds upon the death of the insured person.

Bond A Bond is a certificate or evidence of indebtedness. Corporations, governments and government agencies frequently borrow funds and issue bonds to acknowledge the debt. Interest is usually paid semi-annually in addition to repaying the full amount of the original debt at some future, specified date. The market value of a Bond tends to fluctuate with interest rate changes.

Book Value The Book Value of a share of stock is generally considered to be a corporation's total assets minus its liabilities divided by the number of shares outstanding.

Broker A Broker is an agent who is paid a fee for arranging contracts for the purchase and sale of property.

Buy-Sell Agreement A Buy-Sell agreement is a contract wherein two or more parties agree on terms and conditions under which a designated property may be bought and sold by the parties.

Capital Gain and Capital Loss A Capital Gain or Capital Loss is the respective profit or loss resulting from the sale of a capital asset after comparing the seller's adjusted basis in the asset with the sale price received.

Cash Flow Cash Flow is the sum resulting from an analysis of all changes affecting cash (currency on hand and bank demand deposits) during an Accounting Period.

Cash Value   Cash Value is most frequently associated with certain types of life insurance policies, usually known as whole life policies. A portion of the premiums paid on these policies provides for insurance; the remainder goes into a form of savings also known Cash Value. Cash Value is the same as a policy's loan value.

Certificate of Deposit (CD)   A Certificate of Deposit (usually issued by a bank or banking organization) is a written note promising the purchaser of the note to pay back at a future date the amount of the deposit plus a stated amount of interest.

Charitable Remainder Gift   A Charitable Remainder Gift of property is a type of trust in which the creator of the trust or another named individual receives the income from or holds the right to use the gifted property until death at which time the property remaining passes to a designated charity.

Clifford Trust/Reversionary Trust   A Clifford Trust or a Reversionary Trust are special trusts which last for ten years and a day. Trust property is transferred to the Clifford Trust and income is available for the benefit of the beneficiary. After a specified period of time the property reverts to the original owner.

Closely Held Corporation   A Closely Held Corporation is a corporation with very few stockholders. The stockholders are usually also the officers of the corporation. A family corporation is an example of a Closely Held Corporation.

Codicil   A Codicil is a formally executed addition to or change in the terms of a will not requiring the complete rewriting of the will.

Common Stock   Common Stock is a class of shares *below* or subordinate to any form of Preferred Stock issued by the same corporation. (See Preferred Stock.)

Community Property   Community Property is a concept of property ownership. In a state in which the Community Property principle applies, each partner in a marriage is considered to own one-half of all property accumulated during the marriage by either spouse, except property from inheritance or gifts.

Compound Interest   When interest is computed and credited toward the principal and future interest is then calculated on the sum of principal and interest, it is said to be Compound Interest. Interest is, in effect, paid on interest as well as on principal. (See Interest.)

Contract   A Contract is an agreement between two or more people or institutions (the parties) which is legally binding and enforceable. Not all agreements are contracts.

Convertible Bond   A Convertible Bond is a corporate bond that can be exchanged for a stated number of shares of the same corporation's common stock.

Corporate Bond A Corporate Bond is an evidence of indebtedness issued by a corporation. If the bond is secured it is backed up by certain identified property. If necessary, the secured property may be sold to pay the debt. (See Debenture for details of a general purpose bond.)

Coupon Bond A Coupon Bond is a bond to which Coupons are attached. The Coupons must be removed and remitted to the proper authority for collection of interest due.

Custody Account A Custody (or Custodial) Account occurs when a bank or trust company takes responsibility for the physical protection of a customer's investment certificates for collecting and recording the income from that property on behalf of the customer.

Debenture A Debenture is evidence of indebtedness issued by a corporation. Unlike a secured bond a Debenture is not backed by a specific property. (See Corporate Bond.)

Deed A Deed refers to a document representing ownership of real property.

Depreciation Depreciation is the decrease in value of property. To Depreciate property is to take a deduction reflecting the decreasing value of the property due to deterioration or age.

Dividend A Dividend is that payment received by the owners of a corporation's stock. Dividends are paid from the corporation's profits.

Dollar Cost Averaging Dollar Cost Averaging occurs when systematically investing in stock or a mutual fund. When an individual invests through the dollar cost average method he or she invests a fixed amount at periodic and regular intervals.

Domicile A person's Domicile is his or her principal residence.

Encumber To Encumber is to subject property to a legal claim.

Equity Equity is the amount or value of property not subject to liens or legal claims.

Escheat Escheat is abandoned property reverting to the state.

Escrow Escrow is money held in a trust by a third party until the time of an agreed-upon occurrence.

Estate A person's Estate is all of his or her money and all of his or her real and personal property.

Estate Planning Estate Planning is the process of creating and preserving one's property during one's lifetime and arranging for the property's maximally beneficial transfer at one's death.

Execute Execute is used in two contexts: (1) the act of signing a document, and (2) the act of carrying out the terms of a document.

Executor An Executor is a person bank or trust company named in a will to carry out the terms of the will.

Exempt When income is Exempt from taxes, no tax is due on that income. Interest from municipal bonds, for example, is *exempt* from federal income tax.

Fair Market Value   Assuming all relevant facts about a property are known and the buyer is not forced to buy and the seller not forced to sell, the Fair Market Value of a property is the amount of money a willing buyer would pay for the property to a seller willing to sell it in an arms-length transaction.

Fiduciary   A Fiduciary is a person or institution with the responsibility for acting on behalf of another person.

Fiscal Year   A Fiscal Year is a financial year. The term is often used in reference to taxation. A calendar year ends on December 31 while a Fiscal year may end on the last day of any month.

Fund   *To Fund* is to provide money or property. *A Fund* is a pool of such money or property.

Generation-Skipping Transfer Tax   A Generation-Skipping Transfer Tax resulted when the Tax Reform Act of 1976 altered previous law by introducing a tax on certain transfers of assets *through* the first and on to the second generation heirs of the person who arranged the transfer.

Gift Tax/Gift Tax Exclusion   A gift to an individual or to an organization not qualifying as non-profit, may be subject to a Gift Tax.

A Gift Tax Exclusion applies to annual gifts valued at $10,000 or less from one individual to another as long as the gifts may be used immediately. Such a gift is not subject to a gift tax, and there is no restriction on the number of such gifts to different individuals. The exclusion is $20,000 per year if the gift is given mutually by husband and wife.

Grantor   A Grantor is a person who transfers property to another. The term Grantor is sometimes used synonymously with *trustor,* the person who transfers property in a trust.

Guaranty   A Guaranty is an agreement to perform another person's undertaking should such performance become necessary.

Guardian   A Guardian is a person appointed by the court to control and manage another person's affairs and/or that person's property. A Guardian is usually appointed only in cases of incompetency or minors.

Heir   An Heir is one who is given property either through a will or through state laws regarding the distribution of a decedent's property.

H.R. 10 Plan   Another name for a Keogh Plan.

Hypothecate   To Hypothecate is to pledge property as security for a loan without delivering ownership of the property to the creditor.

Incidents of Ownership   The Incidents of Ownership are often referred to as the *rights* an insured individual has to a life insurance policy without owning the policy. For example, an individual may give his policy to another but retain certain rights to borrow money on or cancel the policy.

Individual Retirement Account An Individual Retirement Account, commonly abbreviated and referred to as an IRA, is a retirement fund set up by an individual for his or her own benefit. The individual makes *tax-deductible* contributions to the IRA out of his own money, and the account earns interest tax-free until retirement.

Installment Sale For federal income tax purposes an Installment Sale of property is a sale of property over a number of years. Under certain conditions the buyer may pay an agreed-upon amount each year, and the seller reports for tax purposes only the proportionate gain from the annual amount received.

Interest—Simple and Compound Interest *Interest* is a payment for the use of money. *Simple Interest* is figured by multiplying the principal amount by the interest rate. For example, the simple interest on $1,000 at 5% would be $50.

Compound Interest involves the number of times the interest rate will be applied over a certain period of time. Interest gained on the first computation is added to the principal amount before the next computation and this process is repeated until the designated period of time is over. (See Compound Interest.)

Inter Vivos Inter Vivos means, literally, between living people. For example, an Inter Vivos gift is a gift from one living person to another.

Intestate To die Intestate is to die without a will.

Invasion of Trust A trust fund is considered Invaded if money is taken from the *principal amount* of the trust.

Inventory At death all of a decedent's property is listed and valued (appraised) for tax purposes. This is known as the Inventory. (See Appraise.)

Joint and Survivor When applied to the ownership of property and its transfer at death, the term Joint and Survivor means the survivor will have rights to some or all of the property at the death of the other owner. *Joint and Survivor* life insurance policies are available.

Joint Ownership Joint Ownership is the shared ownership of property by two or more people.

Judgment In law a Judgment is an official court decision, including in some cases a monetary award to one party for damages.

Jurisdiction Jurisdiction is the geographical region of authority or legal authority of a court.

Keogh Plan (H.R. 10 Plan) A Keogh Plan, also known as an H.R. 10 Plan, is a tax-deductible retirement plan established by a self-employed individual or by a partner in a partnership. The funds contributed to the plan accumulate tax-free each year and are available to the individual at his retirement or, in the case of his death, to his beneficiary.

Leverage   As a financial term Leverage is the control of property without having paid for that property in full. The term is most frequently used in regard to real estate transactions. A Leverage Buyout occurs when an investor acquires control of a business by borrowing against the assets of the business.

Lien   A Lien on a property is a legal claim against it or an encumbrance on it.

Life Estate   A person with a Life Estate in property has a right to use the property during his or a designated other person's lifetime. Such a person is called a Life Tenant.

Line of Succession   In a will the Line of Succession is the instruction as to how property will pass.

Margin   To maintain a Margin account with a stockbroker is to have the ability to purchase securities on credit given by the broker.

Marital Deduction   IRS allows one to leave 100% of one's estate to the surviving spouse before federal estate taxes are calculated, thus the term Marital Deduction.

Money Market/Money Market Fund   The term Money Market describes the trading of short-term certificates of debt—treasury bills and commercial paper, for example.

A Money Market Fund is a type of investment company or mutual fund that purchases various short-term certificates of debt and then sells shares of ownership in the collected portfolio.

Mortgage   A mortgage is a legal claim to real property that serves as security for a loan.

Municipal Bond   A Municipal Bond is a certificate of debt issued by a state or local government or government agency. Generally the interest paid on such bonds is exempt from federal income tax.

Net Worth   A person's Net Worth is the value of properties (assets) minus the amount of indebtedness (liabilities). A *negative net worth* occurs when the liabilities exceed the assets.

Note   As a financial term, a Note is a certificate of indebtedness, sometimes called an IOU.

Open Estate   An Open Estate is an estate still honoring claims by creditors.

Option   As an investment term, an Option is the right to buy property at a certain price for a certain period of time.

Over the Counter (OTC)   Many publicly traded stocks are not listed on a major stock exchange such as the New York or the American Stock Exchanges. When such stocks are bought and sold, they are said to be traded Over The Counter.

Par Value   The Par Value of a bond is the amount of money the issuer promises to pay when the bond matures, also known as the face amount.

Pension Plan   A Pension Plan (often referred to as a defined benefits plan) is a plan, fund or program which provides retirement income to employees when they reach retirement age.

Perpetuity, Rules Against   If something exists in Perpetuity, it exists forever. Trusts with individual beneficiaries are prohibited by law from existing in perpetuity.

Petition for Probate of Will   In some states the request that a will be admitted into probate court is called a Petition For Probate Of Will.

Pledge   To Pledge property is to deliver the property to a creditor as security for a debt.

Portfolio   As a financial term a person's or institution's Portfolio is the total of all investments.

Power of Appointment   Generally, Power of Appointment is the right conferred by one person by will or deed of trust upon another person to designate who will receive the benefit of property, either presently or after those named to receive it in the will or trust agreement have died.

Preferred Stock   Preferred Stock is a class of stock having preference over common stock. In most cases dividends are a stated amount (e.g., 10%) and are payable before dividends may be paid on common stock. (See Common Stock.)

Profit Sharing Plan   Some corporations offer a Profit Sharing Plan (often referred to as a defined contribution plan) to employees as a retirement benefit.

Proxy   To vote by Proxy is to authorize another person or persons to vote in one's place.

Prudent Man Rule   Trustees (as fiduciaries) must manage trust property in accordance with the Prudent Man Rule. The Prudent Man Rule requires the trustees to handle the property with the same care that a prudent, honest, intelligent and diligent man would use to handle the property under the same circumstances.

Redeem/Redemption   To Redeem is to buy back. The Redemption of stock is the repurchase of the stock from the stockholder by the corporation that issued it.

Release   Release is the giving up of a right, claim or privilege by one person to another person against whom the right, claim or privilege might have been demanded or enforced.

Residual Estate   A Residual Estate is what remains of an estate after all claims and taxes have been paid and all distributions have been made.

Return   The Return on an investment is the amount the investment pays to the investor based on the amount invested, usually expressed in terms of percentages.

Revocation of a Will   To Revoke a Will is to make the will ineffective, for example, by making a new will inconsistent with the first.

Safekeeping Account   A Safekeeping Account with a bank is a service through which the bank or trust company takes responsibility for the physical protection of a customer's securities.

Security   As an investment a Security is an evidence of the right to participate in earnings and distribution of property or an evidence of money owed the holder of the security.

Settlement Options   In life insurance, Settlement Options provide for alternate ways by which the value of the life insurance policy may be paid to the beneficiary.

Spendthrift Clause   Also known as Protection from Claims by Strangers, a Spendthrift Clause in a trust agreement provides that the named beneficiary has a right to trust income only and thus cannot voluntarily dispose of the capital assets (principal) of the trust or the income before it is earned and paid.

Statutory Share   A Statutory Share of estate property is a share determined by state law.

Stock Option   A Stock Option is a contracted opportunity to buy stock at a certain price within a certain period of time or before a stated date.

Successor   A Successor is one who follows another in a particular office.

Surety   Surety is a financial guarantee that an act will be carried out or a debt will be paid by another person. To post bond is to provide such surety.

Tax Bracket   For federal tax purposes, an individual's Tax Bracket refers to the level at which income tax rates are applied to his or her annual taxable income.

Tax Shelter   A Tax Shelter is an investment in property designed to reduce the tax liability on income from other sources by providing deductions that can be taken against that other income.

Tax (or Taxable) Year   A Tax Year (or Taxable Year) is that twelve-month period used for the computing of taxes. A tax year is either a *calendar* year ending on December 31 or a *fiscal* year ending on the last day of another month. (See Calendar Year and Fiscal Year.)

Tenant   A Tenant is one who rents space in a building for business or personal use. In broader terms, a tenant is one who owns certain rights to a property such as the right of a joint tenant or life tenant.

Testamentary Capacity   Testamentary Capacity is the legal competence to make a will, such as being of age and mentally competent.

Trust/Trusts   Property in Trust is held and managed by a person or institution (the trustee) for the benefit of those persons or institutions (the beneficiaries) for whom the trust was created. The creator of a trust is commonly referred to as the settlor, grantor or trustor.

Trusts that are created and go into effect while the settlor is still alive are called Living or Inter Vivos Trusts. Trusts established by the settlor in his or her will to go into effect at his death are called Testamentary Trusts.

Trust Agreement   Also known as a trust instrument, deed of trust, or trust indenture, a Trust Agreement is the written document explaining the purpose, provisions and directions of a trust.

Trust Company   A Trust Company specializes in assisting in the creation of trusts and serving as trustee or co-trustee of trusts, and in serving as executor, administrator or guardian of estates.

Trustee   A Trustee is that person or institution named in a trust agreement to hold, care for, manage and distribute trust property.

Trust Fund   A Trust Fund is the principal amount of a trust, the capitol or property in a trust.

Trust Officer   In a trust company or bank trust department, a Trust Officer is that individual responsible for the care of individual trusts.

Trustor   Also known as a settlor, donor or grantor, a Trustor is the creator of a trust.

Vest/Vested Interest   When an individual's right to property becomes Vested, that right is fixed; it cannot be taken away. A Vested Interest in property, then, is a fixed or established right to that property.

Will   A Will is a legal document by which an individual can direct to whom his property will pass at his or her death, how it will pass and by whom it will be managed as it passes. If it is to be approved as legitimate by the probate court, a will must be written in the language and form acceptable under the laws of the state in which the maker of the will lives.

Yield   The Yield of an investment is the amount of money it pays to the owner annually, usually expressed as a percentage of the market value of the investment.